PRAISE FOR RETURN TO THE SCENE OF THE CLIMB

James T. Lester is one of the few persons who saw an expedition to Mount Everest for what it really is, and his craft of telling human stories with honesty and affection makes his book a timeless treasure. It is rare for a westerner to see Sherpas beyond just a number of people assisting his team on the mountain. We could connect with Lester on so many levels, being moved by the human sides of stories that often get overlooked in 'bigger' histories.

— ANKIT BABU ADHIKARI & PRADEEP BASHYAL
AUTHORS OF *SHERPA: STORIES OF LIFE AND DEATH FROM THE FORGOTTEN GUARDIANS OF EVEREST*

In this mini-masterpiece, Jim Lester illuminates the fortitude of a driven team of Americans, then returns to the scene of the climb to explore the trajectories of the Sherpas who made their Everest success possible. The two cultures converge – and find they share a common humanity.

— BROUGHTON COBURN, CONSERVATIONIST,
AUTHOR OF *THE VAST UNKNOWN: AMERICA'S FIRST ASCENT OF EVEREST*

Just as John Morris, a non-climber, was there in 1953 to chronicle Hillary and Tenzing and the British triumph on Everest, James Lester accompanied his countrymen in 1963, as Jim Whittaker became the first American to reach the summit of the world. Unlike Morris, a journalist on the trail of a scoop, Lester was there to study the men, seeking psychological insights in their mental and physical struggles. The diaries, notes, and commentary that make up this wonderful book offer both a unique portrait of the heroic climbers of 1963, and an astonishing opening to a time of innocence when reaching the top of Everest somehow seemed perfectly aligned with dreams to reach the surface of the moon.

— WADE DAVIS, AUTHOR OF *INTO THE SILENCE: THE GREAT WAR, MALLORY AND THE CONQUEST OF EVEREST*

This is a wonderful look at one of the most under-appreciated elements of the adventure life: the way that these experiences can change the lives of everyone involved—especially those local peoples who too often stand in the shadows of adventure stories. It stands out as a unique, insightful, and remarkably compassionate contribution to mountain literature.

— GEOFF POWTER, MOUNTAINEER, AUTHOR OF *STRANGE AND DANGEROUS DREAMS*

RETURN TO THE SCENE OF THE CLIMB

JAMES T. LESTER

EDITED BY
ALISON JEAN LESTER

BENCH PRESS

Copyright © 2023 by Alison Jean Lester.

All rights reserved.

No part of this book may be reproduced in any form or by any electronic or mechanical means, including information storage and retrieval systems, without written permission from the publisher, except for the use of brief quotations in a book review.

For permission requests, write to the publisher via the www.benchpressbooks.com contact page.

ISBN: 978-1-8381124-7-9 (Hardback)

Book design and manuscript photograph by Andrew Gurnett.

Front cover image and all other photographs from the collection of James T. Lester.

Published by Bench Press

www.benchpressbooks.com

CONTENTS

Foreword   xi
by Dr. Pasang Yangjee Sherpa

Another Word   xv
from Tom Hornbein

Introduction   xix
by Alison Jean Lester

PART ONE
JIM'S EVEREST

Cast Of Characters	3
Getting Acquainted	15
The Grand Tour	20
Kathmandu	27
East Toward Everest	31
The Final Approach	43
Conquest Of Chaos	52
Valley Of Silence	61
Assault - I	73
Interlude	84
Assault - II	87
The Return	106
Addendum	124

PART TWO
ROLE REVERSAL

Role Reversal	131
Addendum	154

PART THREE
THE CLASS OF '63

Namche Bazar	159
Khumjung and Kunde	188
Darjeeling	205

Kathmandu	225
Conclusion	237
Further Reading	241
Acknowledgments	243
About the Authors	244

"You may be hearing from the highest-climbing psychologist in the world!"

— JIM LESTER IN A LETTER TO HIS SISTER, JANE, FROM ADVANCE BASE CAMP, APRIL 15, 1963

"I'm so glad we were there when we were."

— TOM HORNBEIN

1998

The sudden view, together with the depressing difficulty of this stretch, brought back to me in a rush the long-forgotten, maybe even repressed, discomforts of the earlier approach to Everest on foot. The comforting ability of memory to simplify and selectively soften the hard edges of the past had allowed me to imagine for decades that I had swanned through here with ease. My senses now said to me clearly, probably not!, as I was forced to recall the terrific blisters that 12 days of walking to this point had generated in 1963; my new expedition boots were completely unbroken-in. Later on this trip it hit me forcefully that on this little Khumbu adventure I experienced again, as if they had been fast-forwarded, some of the significant features, emotional features, of the whole four-month 1963 experience: vague and unreal expectations, shock on encountering the ground-level reality, struggle with negative thoughts, accommodation to the situation, reduction to just putting one foot in front of the other, repeating little mantras like "slow step, short step, closer all the time," and "just keep going." Only a return to the scene of the crime was able to bring back these not-so-pretty memories.

All I really had to work with was the group photograph of our Sherpas taken at the end of the expedition...

FOREWORD
BY DR. PASANG YANGJEE SHERPA

In the summer of 2021, I was piecing together historical information about transnational Sherpas with anthropologist Jim Fisher. We'd heard that some Sherpas from the 1963 American Mount Everest Expedition (AMEE) had taken a road trip across the United States, and our search for details eventually led us to the daughter of the man who was at the wheel, psychologist Jim Lester. Alison and her brother, Toby, generously shared their father's papers with us right away.

I thought we'd be seeing the itinerary of the trip; I could not even imagine that such a detailed chronicle of it could exist, and that I would get a chance to directly engage with it.

Jim Lester drove the men across the country documenting every adventure along the way. He was in charge of their travel arrangements, and became the guide to his guides from the Himalaya. He wrote that he was "their route-planner, chauffeur, interpreter, bill-payer, and, I like to think, comrade; thus, in a sense I became a Sherpa guide." This role reversal gave him an insight into the Sherpa culture as much as it did his own.

Sherpa high-altitude workers have played a crucial role in

enabling great human feats on mountains. However, they are rarely acknowledged, and usually appear nameless in the background. When Sherpas are mentioned in the literature, the patronizing undertone in writings by their Western counterparts is hard to miss. It is also not unusual to see grateful sahibs write about *their* Sherpas without critical self-reflection. In this context, Lester's descriptions are refreshing.

They include accounts of the first days on the road and his observation of how each member was reacting to new experiences. There is a level of sophistication with which he is able to compare his own worldview against those of the Sherpas he interacted with over the course of several months in the 1960s. He acknowledges that during the expedition he was too focused on studying the American team members and their behaviors. In this sense, Sherpas were peripheral to him even though they were everywhere doing what was essential. To be sure, the papers are true to their era. Sherpa men are referred to as boys and their experience in the United States described as a guardian would. But such reflexivity as Lester did possess at the time is rare.

Lester's words spoke to me all these years later because the papers contained personal details about the Sherpa men I could relate to. I could tell that he understood them the way someone can only after spending many days and nights eating and laughing together.

Growing up, I had heard stories about this trip while visiting Khumbu villages. It comes up without fail when someone starts speculating on the introduction of cowboy hats in Sherpa society. *How did cowboy hats and cowboy boots make their way to the Sherpas in Khumbu?* This topic remains half-settled, continuing to make its rounds when Sherpas gather. Now I can see that it is very likely that the three Sherpa men from Khumbu and the two Sherpa men from Darjeeling took these prized items with them from their visit to an American ranch. Lester did not put an end to this debate in his papers, but there are pictures to prove that the Sherpa men had indeed worn cowboy hats and boots on this trip, making it plausible that they introduced them to the Sherpas back home.

What stands out for me, though, is his account of the Sherpa men's experience at a dairy farm. It surprised me because I was not expecting it. Lester was a careful host, always assessing how his guests were doing during their eight-week stay, to find the best American experience for them. He noticed that they did not enjoy this particular visit. What was expected to be an impressive display of technology for extracting a large amount of milk from American cows turned out to be a cold experience for the men because they saw the scene from the cow's point of view. The sight of the animal, plugged unnaturally into all the hoses, troubled their senses. In telling this story, Lester showed how the same world can be viewed in two ways. There is one perspective that centers technology as a means to extract resources from animals and then there is another perspective that centers human-animal relatedness—men capable of empathizing with the cows.

Nearly two years after first reading Lester's observations, I continue to explore what this unexpected gift teaches us about the friendships built on the mountains between the Sherpa hosts and their visiting clients. This is where his papers from 1998, when he conducted interviews with the AMEE Sherpa team members, are instructive. It was clear from this second set of papers that he was committed to understanding Sherpas' perspectives on the immense socio-cultural changes in all of their lives following the historic expedition. Lester had lived with Sherpas on his mind for decades, wanting to give them a platform to voice themselves. I wish so dearly that I had gotten a chance to meet the person. Fortunately for us, we have his words, and Alison has brought them to life.

ANOTHER WORD
FROM TOM HORNBEIN

Our lives first connected as members of the 1963 American Mount Everest Expedition. Norman Dyhrenfurth's dream was to put the first American atop the highest point on Earth a decade after the mountain was first climbed by Edmund Hillary and Tenzing Norgay. In addition, the expedition had a small research component, which is why Jim Lester, a psychologist who had never climbed a mountain in his life, was there: to observe what personality attributes were associated with a group working constructively together in a high risk, high stress endeavor. I was there as a member of the climbing team and as the doctor responsible for the oxygen breathing system used to facilitate climbing back in those days.

During our months on the mountain, Jim somewhat nervously ascended the Icefall to spend weeks ensconced at 21000-foot Advanced Base Camp in the Western Cwm. He was a caring presence who provided counsel to various members of the team in addition to his research pursuits. He and my tentmate/ropemate Willi Unsoeld bonded, enjoying hours of conversation.

For me, our expedition did not end when we returned to our

homes in June 1963. Everest led to precious friendships, particularly with Jim and with my West Ridge teammate, Barry Corbet. The seeds planted during our days hanging out together on the mountain ripened slowly, blossoming almost four decades later.

Jim returned from Everest as enthusiastic about not climbing mountains as he was before. Despite language barriers, he bonded with the Sherpas in a way we climbers, focused on the top of the mountain, did not. As a result, he ended up escorting five Sherpas and one Nepali liaison officer across the U.S. in a large station wagon during July and August 1963. He even accompanied them to the top of the Grand Teton, a not at all shabby once-in-a-lifetime summit. This time spent together was a major catalyst to his solo return to Nepal 35 years later to find out what had become of them. Jim's account of that venturesome solo journey back to the Solu Khumbu is part of what you are about to read.

When I reflect on what our Everest junket did to and for Jim, I have to conclude that it brought about the major pivotal event in his life. That event was meeting a captivating airline stewardess, Valerie Browne, on Pan Am 1, his flight home from New Delhi (see Valerie Lester's *Fasten Your Seatbelts! History and Heroism in the Pan Am Cabin*). They embarked upon a life journey together, part of which was to produce two more writers, Toby and Alison. Jim's one previous book, *Too Marvelous for Words: The Life and Genius of Art Tatum*, resulted from his own passion for music. He was a talented jazz pianist and trombonist.

Over those after-Everest years, abetted by decadal reunions of the team and a kindred curiosity, Jim and I grew close. Among moments that glow:

A visit by Jim and Val to Kathy's and my home near Seattle, crowned by a wander through Cascade forests to a worthy waterfall.

Our 40th AMEE reunion, which occurred four years early because our numbers were dwindling, best not to put it off. About half of our team of 20 had departed by then. We gathered at Shrine Mountain lodge near Vail Pass in September 1999, the year after Jim's Sherpa search. One of our team sought Jim out, wanting to explore lingering feelings of not contributing to the climbing effort after Jake Breitenbach's death in the Icefall. I was invited to join them in what proved to be a fruitful conversation, and one more precious bond.

Jim and I explored many things, including his research findings, the pieces you are about to read, and his curiosity about what makes climbers tick. But our relationship was not just Jim and me; it very much enfolded our ropemates in the climb of life, Val and Kathy.

On April 14, 2010, his freedom greatly limited by ALS (also known as Lou Gehrig's Disease), Jim embarked on the fast that would end his life some days later. Val, Toby, Alison, and Jim's sister Jane gathered with him for those final days. I chatted by phone with Jim from Seattle each day as long as he was able. Six years before, I had been with Barry Corbet, our Everest teammate, and his family for what I now refer to as do-it-yourself-dying, and had shared that precious experience with Jim. The concept of heroes was a topic that Barry and I, then Jim and I enjoyed exploring. For me, both are heroes, and no less so Val, providing a loving belay until Jim's last breath.

In July 2017, Val came to visit us in our Estes Park, Colorado home, the place I first discovered mountains at age 13. We hiked an unkempt, rocky trail to the top of Prospect Mountain, sat on a granite grandstand, gazing at the peaks of the Continental Divide, watching ravens soar, listening to Anna Gregory singing "Prelude to a Kiss", accompanied on the piano by . . . Jim Lester.

Val died of metastatic melanoma in 2019, one more lesson for me in just letting nature and time take their course. Her exit nine years after Jim's is poignantly captured in Alison's memoir, *Absolutely Delicious: A Chronicle of Extraordinary Dying*.

As I creak into my tenth decade, I know that what Barry and Jim gifted me is tranquility regarding my impending exit, while savoring the richness of each passing day. I know that, should I need to, I have two precious role models of how to exit, simply shutting my mouth for a last handful of days with loved ones around me—tears, hugs, laughter.

I invite you now to savor Jim's journey, a tipping point adventure that changed his life and enriched the lives of many others. I'm one.

INTRODUCTION
BY ALISON JEAN LESTER

All my life, I've had this conversation:

> Me: My father participated in the first American expedition to Mount Everest in 1963.
> Them: (wonderment on face) Wow! Did he make it to the top?
> Me: No. (quickly before their face can fall completely) But he wasn't trying to. He went as a psychologist studying the climbers.
> Them: (wonderment satisfyingly back on face) Wow!

A conversation I've had less frequently, hardly ever in fact until these last few years, is one where I announce that in February 1998, 35 years after that historic climb and now aged 70, my father went on a solo expedition back to Nepal to find as many Sherpas as he could from the 1963 team and discover what their lives had become.

On route home to Maryland from that trip, my father washed up at the little one-bedroom apartment I shared in Tokyo with my first husband and our two very small children. He was exhausted. Dazed.

We didn't know it at the time, but a case of walking pneumonia was brewing in his chest. I was busy, breast-feeding, self-involved. Surely we talked about what the trip had been like for him. I do remember him telling me how nice it was to be able to gobble candy bars without guilt for energy while trekking, and describing some long, cold, fog-bound days waiting for a break in the weather. But I don't remember much else; I think I was mostly relieved to have a babysitter.

Also, it probably didn't feel like a huge deal that he'd just been to Nepal. He'd been before, after all. What's more, I was living in Japan after stints in China, Italy, and Taiwan. My brother had been an English-teacher in Yemen and a UN refugee-affairs officer on the West Bank. My British mother had spent her childhood in Jamaica, and my parents had met on a plane between New Delhi and Beirut. We Lesters went places.

Dad wasn't a mountaineer, though. He wasn't any sort of athlete, or even a hobbyist sportsman. He loved to sit, and especially to lie down, and it drove my energetic mother wild. When I was a young teenager and said I'd like to give mowing the lawn a try, she told me that I shouldn't because it would be bad for my ovaries. I believed her, only to find out decades later that she'd said it to make sure that Dad kept mowing it himself, for his health.

James T. Lester, Jr., known as Jim, was born in 1927 and brought up in St. Louis by Methodist parents keen to keep up with the Joneses, as devoted to their cocktails as to their creator. He was both an introvert and shy. I have a letter here that he wrote to his sister in February 1959, when he was 32 and she was 26. They had clearly both visited their parents for Christmas (he from Los Angeles, where he had completed a PhD in psychology and philosophy, and she from Paris), and neither of them had received a letter from their father since. They wondered why. Dad told her, "I think it may be true that in some way we fell below what he expected from us in the way of behavior and attitude." He also told her about a talk he had with their father after she left:

We discussed quite directly my feeling that he frequently criticized me rather than show pleasure, etc. And I found him quite rigid and angered by this, but at the same time unwilling to admit that it affected him emotionally at all, to have me say that. It did me some good, I must say, just to say it to him, even though I don't think anything really good resulted from it. It may even have been depressing to him. I remember he said something about never having guessed that I was in some ways afraid of people (shy, is the usual word, but I thought he was insightful enough to realize that most shy people are simply afraid).

My dad's all there in that letter, barring his lovely sense of humor. He sticks up for himself a little bit, doesn't expect much to come of it, and thinks through the permutations of the situation, considering all the possibilities.

Dad was a data-gatherer and a dreamer. He developed hypotheses. He told a good story, but never loudly, and never held the floor. People loved having him at a party because of what a wonderful listener he was, and if there was a piano he could be relied upon to play. By profession always a psychologist of some sort or another—clinician, researcher, professor, grant-proposal assessor, he expressed himself most publicly in music, being a very talented jazz pianist and trombonist. He'd begun playing with local jazz groups in St. Louis at 14, and at 19 was writing arrangements for the Army jazz band at Camp Lee, Virginia. He took beautiful, interesting photographs, often of moments or scenes whose power over him he couldn't fully understand in the moment and wanted to look at again later.

But in 1961 he was signed on to the first American Mount Everest Expedition (AMEE). He climbed to 10,000 feet on Mount Rainier in September 1962 when the team gathered to train and try out equipment, he climbed to over 21,000 feet on Everest, and also summitted Grand Teton (13,775 feet) in 1963. Then he never climbed again.

What a story.

Fortunately, he wrote it down.

The first part of this book is his description of the climb, written as a manuscript for young readers (I think he was imagining the middle grades, but as he had difficulty talking down to children, I can't be sure). I didn't know about this manuscript, whose first draft was written a year before I was born, until after he died in 2010, when my mother unearthed it from a closet. It was and still is in an old manila envelope worn to the texture of chamois, torn all down one side and missing most of its curling flap. Inside the envelope is a buff folder with "1965 – draft children's book" on the tab. There are two drafts inside. The first one bears evidence of repeated read-throughs, with corrections and notes variously in graphite pencil, red pencil, and black pen. The second has been given a title page—that must have felt so good!—although after that is a page that simply says

INTRODUCTION
(TO BE WRITTEN)

Introductions are difficult. I have no idea what he was planning for that. He may have wanted to see if he could interest a publisher and get a kick in the pants from them before attempting it.

He didn't write on this draft. The penciled notes on it were made in 1965 by Tom Hornbein and then in 2010 by my mother before she transcribed it onto her computer.

Mum emailed the manuscript to my brother and me in 2010, and I know I read it then. I don't remember how I felt about it, though. (This is getting to be an embarrassing pattern.) Ten years later and between fiction-writing projects, I realized that 2023 was the 60th anniversary of AMEE, and that I had something special to offer the world.

Re-reading it, I found myself as dazzled as if I'd never read it before; as if I hadn't attended Dad's frequent slideshows and talks on the climb throughout my childhood. I'd forgotten the stories, and

Everest had become a rather friendly presence, reduced by the projection screen to a size that could comfortably sit on the couch. I had heard and said the word 'Everest' so often that it had come to feel like an element of our name: Leverester.

"Dad did *that*?" was my constant question as I read. "*My* dad?"

The manuscript is a chronicle of the climb from a very particular and unusual viewpoint for that period of mountaineering—that of an apprentice. As James Ramsey Ullman mentioned about Dad in *Americans on Everest: The official account of the ascent led by Norman G. Dyhrenfurth*, "his blisters had been the worst of all." That's what makes it so interesting, I think, and probably even if you're not his daughter. But he wrote his story of Everest in the middle of the 1960s, and it shows. There are hyphens in strange places, and I'm also leaving the words he underlined for emphasis as they are, rather than italicizing them in the current fashion, to remind you that he wrote this manuscript on a typewriter. Those things may be distracting, but they are cute. More troublingly, there are uncomfortable aspects to the content. All climbers are referred to as men; likewise astronauts, submariners, and Arctic researchers. Also, as Margaret K. McElderry of Harcourt, Brace & World wrote to him in February 1969, having read the manuscript, "the Sherpas ... are given too secondary a role it seems to me, particularly those who actually took part in the climb."

She made an extremely important point.

The daughter in me wants to cry out, "But only Gombu spoke English well enough to hold a conversation, and *he* was busy with Jim Whittaker preparing for the first summit attempt! And Dad was there to study the American climbers! And look at what he wrote to his sister on March 23 from Gorakshep!"

> The Sherpas are a fantastic bunch of people. Strong (and of course used to living at about 14,000 feet) and extremely good-natured and willing to work, they take good care of us and are very pleasant to have along. Their physical capacities, developed at high alti-

tudes, are intimidating to the climbers, who tend to feel that the Sherpas are better qualified than they to climb Mt. Everest. Luckily they seem to be much more motivated to help us do it than to do it themselves – with the exception of <u>one</u> Sherpa we have who is <u>really</u> out to make the summit. And it appears that if anyone can, <u>he</u> will.

I ask myself, if the Sherpas had spoken enough English to tell their stories to Dad, would he have included that in his account of the climb? Well, I don't just like to think he would have; I know it. Because I have two more manuscripts to share with you.

The first is short, a chronicle of an eight-week drive he took across the United States right after AMEE with five of the principal Sherpas and the Nepalese liaison officer from the expedition. He did give at least one slideshow about this road trip, but not many. You'll see in his story of the climb that he knows going to Everest changed his life forever, but this subsequent journey changed it profoundly as well. In its way, it was momentous. Jim Whittaker may have been the first American to get to the top of Everest, but Jim Lester was the first American to travel with the first group of Sherpas to cross the United States.

The third manuscript I have for you is what Dad wrote once he had recovered from his trip to Nepal and Darjeeling in 1998. I also didn't know about this manuscript until after he died. (Are you getting the picture of how quiet he was?) Having now opened all his related computer files, I have learned that he was planning a book, for which he wrote several introductions but this time no conclusion. Conclusions are difficult too, and can also wait until an editor has seen the rest of the work. But as far as I know, no editor did.

I'm the editor now, and as editor I've cut the first few chapters of that manuscript. They sought to bring readers up to date on the history of the Sherpas, their involvement in trekking, and attitudes toward them. A handful of paragraphs from the first chapter are sufficient to lay out his goals:

INTRODUCTION

This ... is not another expedition story. There are enough accounts of such expeditions (for example our 1963 expedition alone spawned three books, at least one of them now a mountaineering classic). But within the stories of expeditions one can often glimpse a crowd of obscure figures, mostly in the shadows of the climbers and of the mountain, figures who are absolutely essential to the plot but who seldom get more than a few sentences in expedition narratives. These are the Sherpas, and they deserve more.

In February of 1998, exactly 35 years after our expedition hit the trail to Everest, I returned to Nepal, to interview as many of those Sherpas who were part of the 1963 American Everest expedition as I could find, and to try to see our expedition in the context of their on-going lives. I wanted, finally, to get a three-dimensional picture of Sherpas.

The word Sherpa, somewhat exotic to Western ears only a few decades ago, is now almost a household word (although recently, when I mentioned to someone that I was "writing a book about Sherpas," she replied, "OK, who is Sherpas?"). Somehow the word has caught on. It has a certain panache, and it has been picked up by a variety of manufacturers and other organizations hoping to promote an image of their product as strong and reliable (as one would want a good porter to be). There is a bag available for carrying small animals on airplanes called the Sherpa Bag, L.L. Bean offers a Sherpa coat, and there is a software program for managing projects called Sherpa. There is even a military fighter plane officially named The Sherpa, and I've heard recently that the aides-de-camp to high-level attendees at an international summit conference are now commonly referred to as Sherpas. Essential, but mostly invisible.

Sherpas on mountaineering expeditions have gotten almost all the publicity, even though they constitute a minority of the Sherpa population in Nepal and India. As a result, the word is almost synonymous with 'porter,' and calls up an image of a sturdy but dim peasant willing to trudge up a mountain with a heavy load.

Sherpa (with a small s) has rapidly become the name of a job, not a people. Granted that carrying goods around in the mountains has been one of their main life-tasks since long before the first mountaineers appeared. Nevertheless, 'Sherpa' does not merely mean 'porter,' and to equate them seems a degradation of an honorable name. The fact is almost lost that the word (spelled with a capital S) identifies an intelligent, adaptable and enterprising ethnic group nourished by an ancient Buddhist tradition and living happily in the Everest region and elsewhere long before Everest became a focus of the world's attention. You might say my aim in this book is to put the capital S back in 'sherpa.'

The rest of that chapter would have been very interesting information to have gathered in one place 25 years ago, but today it is at the touch of your fingertips and on Netflix. I'm going to let you look into the history of the Sherpas yourselves if you're keen to, keeping the last part of this book focused on what you can't find elsewhere: my father's direct experience of finding and interviewing as many of what he called "the class of '63" as he could by walking his aged legs around Solukhumbu and Darjeeling, seven months before the founding of Google.

That's the case for all of this book, in fact: you can't find it elsewhere. Dad was a non-climber who participated in the first American expedition to Everest; an expedition team-member who became sherpa to a group of Sherpas; a grandfather who returned to the foothills of Everest 35 years later out of a sense both of intense and fond curiosity and also, frankly, of shame.

Quiet as he may have been, no one has ever done quite what my father did.

Dad organized his slides by number only. I have done my utmost to correctly identify the people and places in the photographs. Any mistakes are mine entirely.

PART ONE
JIM'S EVEREST
1963

CAST OF CHARACTERS

To get the most from a drama, you should know a little something about each of the characters before the events actually begin. In our American Everest drama, there were twenty in the cast, which is a lot of people to meet at one time. Perhaps if I sort them into two groups it will help.

There were fifteen men on the team who were there mainly to climb and not for any other reason. And there were five of us with other purposes and with no hopes of being among those to reach the actual summit of Everest. Meet these last five first.

The unhopefuls

Jimmy Roberts, an Englishman, was the only team member who was not an American. His job was to hire the porters and Sherpas and to supervise the carrying of our supplies over the 185 miles of hills to Base Camp and from there to the higher camps. As a British army officer who had served in that part of the world for many years, and who had helped train the Nepalese army, he knew the language very well and could give orders and understand difficulties quickly, something none of the rest of us could do. His job may not sound as dramatic as that of the men who pitted their strength against the mountain, but there is no question that Jimmy did as much as anyone to make the climbing of Mt. Everest by Americans possible. If you will look at some of the pictures of our army of porters, and try to imagine that you were responsible for knowing where all the supplies were every night, for keeping things organized so that everyone stuck to one plan, and for getting everything the team would need all the way to Base Camp and then beyond, you will see what I mean!

There was <u>Maynard Miller</u>, who certainly had the strength and the experience to climb as a team-member, but who was along only to carry out some research. Maynard has spent his life studying mountains and glaciers, those rivers of snow and ice that often form on high mountains. From a study of glaciers you can learn a lot about the kinds of weather the area has had in past years, even in past centuries, about chemicals that were in the air in the past, and about the way glaciers form and grow and die with the passing of time. Few people have made such a study of the glaciers on or near Mt. Everest, and Maynard was on the team to help fill in that gap in our knowledge of the earth's surface.

Maynard's work required him to use some measuring instruments. For example, there was a gravity meter (yes, you can actually measure gravity, and what is even more surprising is that it is different in different places!); there were long screws for drilling deep holes into the ice and measuring its temperature (it is warmer close to the surface, colder down deep); and a lovely crystal ball for measuring the amount of sunshine each day. To help him carry and use all of this, Maynard brought along an assistant, the youngest man on the team, <u>Barry Prather</u>. Large and very strong, gentle and friendly, inclined to move slowly but also able to delight the Sherpas (and us) by climbing around on the limbs of a big tree, hanging upside down, this Barry (there were three on the expedition) was known to the team as "Bear." The Sherpas came to call him "Balu," which means the same thing. Bear, too, had the experience to serve as a climber if necessary, but was along mainly to help Maynard with his studies of the ice.

<u>Jim Ullman</u> (James Ramsey Ullman) has long loved mountains, and has written a number of books about them and about the men who show the somewhat mysterious urge to climb them at the risk of their lives. He and Norman Dyhrenfurth, the leader of our expedition, had met 20 years ago, when Norman was a ski instructor and gave Jim some of his first climbing lessons. After every big expedition, one or more of the team members writes a book about it, and our expedition leader wanted the official book describing our effort to be something special. It was a big disappointment to everyone when Jim developed a medical problem in his leg just before we left the United States. He was allowed to fly to Nepal but not to do any hiking. It was his unhappy lot to have to sit for three months in a hotel in Kathmandu while the rest of the team moved out into the countryside and up Mt. Everest, and to have to tell the story of it without getting to see it himself.

I was the fifth man who went for some reason other than to lend strength to the climbing. In my case too the reason was research. As a psychologist, I was along to see whether or not I could learn anything about differences among men—differences in the way they could stand up to the difficult conditions we would find on the mountain, differences in the way they got along with each other, differences in the friends they chose, and such matters as these.

There was a very practical reason for studying these things. There are times when a group of men must be chosen, a group who will be sent into unpleasant places to work under many difficulties. For example, the Navy sends men to the South Pole to live for a year in ice-houses, without their families, without any place to go outside of where they live, where the temperature often goes so low that a man can freeze to death just walking 50 yards to another house, and where no one can reach them all through the winter in case anything should go wrong. In a group of men living in such a place, one man who gets angry too easily, or one who gets so sad and homesick that he makes others blue or cannot do his job, or a man who has habits and ways of doing things that upset others—in other words, a man who just adds to the problems of living and working in such a place, can be a very definite handicap, and it is important to learn how to recognize such people before they are sent to the Antarctic.

Nor do you have to go to the South Pole to meet such problems. In submarines with atomic power, which can travel enormous distances without having to stop anywhere for fuel, the crews are sometimes under the ocean's surface, unable to leave their small quarters or change the faces they have to look at every day, for months on end. Here again, a "sour tomato" in the bunch can make everyone's life miserable, and could even affect the running of the submarine and endanger lives. And now that scientists are learning to make bigger and better rockets, it seems certain that space capsules will grow larger and larger, and will soon carry, not one man or two, but five, ten, possibly even twenty into space at one time. Even a fairly small rocket costs a huge amount of money, and each time one blasts off it is terribly important that nothing should go wrong. Not only must the machinery work perfectly, but the men inside must keep their heads, stay in control of their emotions, cooperate with each other, and get the job done properly that they were sent into space to do. Once again, anything we can learn about what sort of man tends to rub other people the wrong way, or how to recognize a man who will be a handicap rather than an asset, will be worth something to groups like the Navy or the Space Administration, who have to pick the men to be sent to the Pole, to be put on a submarine crew, or to soar into space.

<u>The hopefuls</u>

Setting aside these five, we are left with a climbing team of fifteen men. These are the ones on whose legs, lungs, backs, hearts, and wills the success or failure of the Expedition would depend.

These are the ones who had been climbing since they were 12 or 13 usually, the ones who had been reading about Everest and dreaming of what it might be like—how high, how steep, how cold, how beautiful—for years, almost the way you or I might read about the moon now. To most of them, Chomolungma—the Tibetan name for the mountain we call Everest—had always seemed incredibly far away and hard to get to, some very desirable place that they would never see. And they envied the few men who <u>had</u> seen it, and wondered what they might be like, and whether or not they might be made of the same kind of stuff as those men—those truly remarkable men who had forced their way into the "forbidden" land of Tibet, just to see Everest with their own eyes and try it with their own legs. You can imagine that to be selected to go on this American Expedition was like nothing else that happens in one's life—a chance not only to leave everyday life for a while, to mix with exciting and foreign people on the way over (Japanese, Chinese, Siamese, Indian, and Nepalese), a chance to spend weeks hiking through very beautiful hills and valleys and swim in bitter-cold mountain streams and eat under the stars every night (when it wasn't raining) and never use a bathroom. It was all these things, and too many more to tell in one book. But perhaps most important of all for this band of men it was a chance for each to try himself out, to test his physical strength and his willpower and "push". It was a chance to test himself against a really high standard and find out how he measured up. And it was a chance to make a dream come true, something people don't often succeed in doing.

But obviously there are many more than fifteen men in America who would like to have the chance to try to climb Mt. Everest, and maybe to stand on a little point of land which looks down on everything else in the world. And there are many more than fifteen who are the right age (not too young and not too old), who have the strength and endurance, and who have learned the necessary skills and know what to do in different situations in the mountains. You may ask, why was the number of men on our team just fifteen—why not two, or thirty-five, or a hundred and ten?

First of all, there is a limit to how big an expedition can be. It depends largely on how much money the expedition has; for each additional man on our trip, for example, the cost to the expedition was roughly $10,000 [equivalent to about $97,000 in 2023]. But another thing is that if there are too many men on the team, the group becomes a <u>crowd</u> rather than a <u>team</u>. Then it is harder to climb well, no one knows exactly what he is supposed to do, and everything is less fun and frequently less successful. Climbing Everest in a crowd would be something like playing baseball with twice as many athletes as you need on each side.

On the other hand, it is possible to have too few men on the team. Twice, single climbers have attempted Mt. Everest alone. Neither of them succeeded, and one of them died and froze on the mountain and was not found for several years. For a man with a really huge ambition to prove what he can do, with no one to help him, the dream of climbing Everest alone can be very strong—just as the idea of running a mile faster than anyone ever has, or breaking the speed record at the Indianapolis "500", is very strong for some people. All climbers like to do some climbing alone once in a while, but almost all agree that Everest is not the place to do it. For the really big mountains—and it is hard to give a good impression of how much bigger mountains like Everest are than anything you can find in America—the ideal team is probably between 8 and 16 men. No one can say for sure; it depends on what you want to accomplish.

The man who got this team together and made it possible for us all to go, Norman Dyhrenfurth, had high hopes. Everest is one of three mountains that stand close together, almost forming a U. Norman hoped when we left that the team would reach the summits of all three peaks, Lhotse and Nuptse as well as Everest. All three had been climbed before, but never by one expedition. For this, he would need a fairly large team. As it turned out, our goals changed when we got there and we never attempted Lhotse or Nuptse, but there was plenty for the 15 to do and in the end, we climbed Everest not once, or even twice, but three times!

Once Norman knew about how many men he needed, there still was the problem of how to choose just fifteen out of all the ones that might have been good team members. What he did first was to go to his own personal friends who were climbers and ask them to suggest climbers—men they had climbed with and knew to be good as climbers and also good as companions. Then he asked <u>his</u> friends to ask <u>their</u> friends to suggest more, and in this way he finally found himself with nearly 100 names. He wrote to people who knew each of these men, asked for opinions about them, and visited many of the candidates himself, in different parts of the country. He considered everything he heard about each man, talked it over with the second leader of the Expedition, Will Siri, and finally settled on his team.

Expedition leader Norman Dyhrenfurth

<u>Norman Dyhrenfurth.</u> Aged 44 when we left, Norman earns his living by making motion pictures and teaching others how to. He came to the United States from Switzerland as a young man, and was once a ski-instructor. He had been on or near Everest three times before. It was his dream to put an American team on the summit, and it was the years of work he gave to getting people to give the money and finding the team that made the trip possible for the rest of us. I wanted to call him by the name of Li'l Abner's hero, "Fearless Fosdick", because of his very strong jaw-line.

<u>Will Siri.</u> (42) Will is a scientist studying the way things work inside the body. Norman chose him as second leader because he liked him and because Will had been leader of his own expedition to the Himalayas some years before (a mountain called Makalu). Will is a very quiet man, smokes a pipe a lot, and you usually can't tell what he's thinking about. It makes you wonder if he's a little shy. Besides

being Norman's "lieutenant" he also did research on how the body works at such great altitudes.

<u>Willi Unsoeld.</u> (36) Willi usually is a college teacher but in 1963 was in the Peace Corps in Nepal. He was one of the climbers with the longest experience and the best reputation. Many people knew his name, even if they didn't know him personally, because climbers often talked about the climbs he had done and what an interesting person they thought he was. He likes people very much, and especially likes to help others, listening to their problems, helping them make up their minds when they don't know what to do, cheering them up when they feel moody. He had the loudest laugh of all of us. He too had been in the Himalayan mountains before, and although he didn't have the title of "leader" many of the team expected him to be one.

<u>Dick Pownall.</u> (35) Dick teaches physical education and mathematics in high school in Denver. Another of the most experienced climbers in the group, he was the first man to climb a rock wall in the Teton mountains that is almost all straight up and that looks as though no one could ever do it. He is another very quiet man, but it probably isn't shyness. He just doesn't think it is worthwhile to say much unless it is very important or very useful to someone. He took better care of himself—washing, changing socks, and things like that —than many of us did, and he was very confident that Mt. Everest would not be too hard to climb.

<u>Jim Whittaker.</u> (34) Jim (whom we called "Big Jim") runs a sporting goods store in Seattle. Whittaker looks more like a mountaineer than anyone else, since he is very tall and you can see even with a suit on that he has done a lot of exercising to build up his muscles. He has guided a lot of people up Mt. Rainier, he has escaped from some snow avalanches, and his name is often in the papers around Seattle. He is a very friendly fellow, and he likes to make other people laugh.

<u>Barry Bishop.</u> (31) Barry is another one who has been near Mt. Everest before. He works for the National Geographic Society, taking

pictures and writing articles for the magazine, and he took pictures for them on the Expedition. He is a little shorter than many of the others, and a little wider, and everyone called him "Barrel" but he didn't seem to mind it. He has a lot of energy, and he also has quite a temper, but it usually does down again very quickly. He tells a lot of jokes and many of them would embarrass girls, but it seemed all right out in the mountains. Later I'll explain how he lost all of his toes on our Expedition.

<u>Dick Emerson.</u> (37) Dick teaches college, and has been climbing and guiding for a long time. He has a very gentle, easy manner, even though he is very strong, especially in his legs. There was a lot of planning needed to make sure that enough food, and enough oxygen and other equipment, would be carried to each of the camps, and Dick did most of that planning, which was a job that not many wanted to do. He also was doing some psychological research on the climb, but it didn't keep him from being a climber, too.

<u>Gil Roberts.</u> (28) Gil is young, but looks and in some ways acts older. He is a doctor, which means that he hasn't had the time some of the others have had to build up lots of climbing experiences, but he is no stranger to mountains either. Along with Dave Dingman, he was in charge of keeping everyone as healthy as possible. He didn't want to encourage us to "see the doctor" though, and it was impossible to get any sympathy from him for the various pains and miseries that we felt. He was another one with a temper, and he looked like he was irritated more often than he really was. When there was a real emergency, however, he took over and handled things perfectly. Dick Pownall later called him a "hero".

<u>Dave Dingman.</u> (26) one of the youngest men on the team, also a doctor, had the job of helping Roberts with medical problems. You couldn't get any sympathy out of him either, but he saved Bear's life at about 24,000 feet, and did his share as a climber as well. At home he was something of a ladies' man—good-looking, well-dressed, and "smooth"—but on the mountain his hair grew longer, and his beard grew shaggier, than almost anyone else's. And he wore the same

tattered and torn red shirt the whole time; by the time the return march was over, the shirt was little more than a rag hanging out of his belt and dragging behind him.

Tom Hornbein. (32) Tom was the third medical man on the team, but health was not his job on this trip the way it was for Roberts and Dingman. Instead, Tom was responsible for everything having to do with the oxygen we took along. He even designed a new kind of oxygen mask which turned out to be better than anything ever used in the mountains before. Hornbein is a tiny man compared to the rest of the team, and very wiry and muscular, with practically no fat on him. He talks softly, but when he has made up his mind to do something, there is no way to stop him. And although he looks too small to be much good on a monstrous mountain such as Everest, as it turned out he had as much push and power as anyone—if not more than anyone.

Lute Jerstad. (27) Lute, a young but very powerful climber with a strong will, is studying to be a college teacher, and is especially interested in everything that has to do with the theater—he has even acted in some plays himself. In a way, that's strange because the theater is such an indoor thing and Jerstad is such an outdoor person. You look at him and you think he is made just for sports and hard work. But talk to him and you find he is interested in learning and thinking as well. He is a very jolly, merry man, who usually cheered everyone up when he was around. He likes to see people enjoying themselves, and often would recite funny poems just when we were dragging ourselves up a long, hot hill that seemed endless, when we needed something to laugh at. Lute and Tom kidded each other very day about who was really the uglier. I tried not to take sides.

Dan Doody. (29) Dan was a student of making motion pictures and very good at it, and one of the best rock-climbers in the group. He was a long, thin man with a dark beard even before we left, and he reminded me of boys you sometimes see in cartoons, making whiskey by moonlight in some Arkansas forest. He didn't actually do that, but he <u>did</u> make his own beer at home, and also something called <u>mead</u> which is like beer with lots and lots of honey in it and very thick. Like Lute, he was another man who looked pretty rough and unpolished on the outside but who was very thoughtful on the inside. He never had much to say out loud and when he tried to make jokes they often weren't very funny. But when Jim Ullman read his diary after the expedition, he said he found it more interesting and better written than most of the others, and showed that he might have become a good writer some day. Unfortunately, and everyone on the Expedition has been very saddened by this, two years after the end of our adventure Dan was climbing on a high rock wall in Vermont and slipped off, falling to his death. Climbers often run the danger of such a thing, but every time it happens it is sad. It was especially sad that it happened to Dan, because every year of his life seemed to be getting better. But at least no wife and children were left without a husband and father, because Dan was the only unmarried climbing member of the team.

<u>Al Auten.</u> (36) Al is a magazine editor and a "ham" radio operator, and knows a lot about radios and engines. He was in charge of one big radio so that we could talk to people several hundred miles away in case we needed help, and also of the little walkie-talkies we used to talk to each other when we were at different camps along the way. Another quiet one, he didn't have much confidence that other people would like him. As it turned out, he played a very useful part as a strong climber as well as radio-man.

<u>Jake Breitenbach.</u> (27) Jake was a slim blond man who ran a ski shop in Jackson, Wyoming, and had done a lot of summer guiding in the Teton Mountains there. He always seemed to keep what he was thinking very private, and no one except his old and good friend Barry Corbet ever got to feel that they knew him very well. He was very appealing in a strange way. When I looked over my photographs, I found I had taken more shots of him than of anyone else during the long trip to Nepal, and in many of them he had a very wistful, far-away look, the kind of look that makes you want to know

what's on the person's mind—but with Jake you almost never found out. He died on the mountain; it was the only death we had—although there were two other close calls.

<u>Barry Corbet.</u> (27) Barry runs a ski-lodge in Wyoming. He does some mountain-guiding in the summer and some ski-instructing in the winter, and he is known as one of the better young rock-climbers in the United States. He is another man who is strong and gentle at the same time—an athlete who is also very thoughtful and interested in learning. I never saw him get mad at anyone—if he did, he hid it very well, and usually seemed in a good mood. In fact, the closer we got to the high mountains, the happier he seemed, and his eyes began to shine like someone in love. He was quite good at knowing what other people were thinking or feeling, and for that reason the others felt close to him. He was Jake's best friend, and his opinion—that Jake died at a time when he was as happy as he had ever been in his life—helped the rest of us to live with that death.

But I'm getting ahead of the story...

GETTING ACQUAINTED

Usually, an expedition consists of three or four, possibly as many as eight or ten, climbers who all know each other and have done small climbs together. Out of their weekend experiences with each other comes the decision to go off for a longer time and tackle a bigger challenge than their local hills and rocks can provide. But our Expedition didn't start this way. Instead, the idea of climbing Mt. Everest came first, and the selection of the men to do it came second.

Among our twenty there were quite a number who didn't know each other at all. Although every man had been highly recommended as being able to get along with others, still it seemed a good idea that we should all meet before we left the United States. At least then we wouldn't have to waste time later "breaking the ice," when there were more important things to do.

Also, for so large a team there was a huge amount of equipment to be bought—sleeping bags, tents, parkas, hiking pants, climbing pants, ice-axes, and right on down to gloves and socks—not to mention the tons of food we would need. Each man had his own ideas—about what kind of equipment would be the best for us, what kind of tent he would feel the safest in, what kind of boot he could depend on to protect his feet, what kind of food he could eat for three and a half months—and so another reason for getting together before we left was to discuss all these things, try out different items, and arrive at choices that everyone could agree on.

Five months before our departure (which was to be on February 3, 1963) we gathered from all over the country, meeting in Seattle at "Big Jim" Whittaker's house. Most of us stayed with him, sleeping in the basement or on the lawn in borrowed sleeping bags, eating sandwiches and drinking beer for most meals. Jim lives on a lake, and we were able to do a little swimming and water-skiing for a few days before we went up to Mt. Rainier. The town knew that we were there, and there were television appearances, press conferences, honorary breakfasts, and the like, and all in all it was a busy, exciting time. Just meeting our fellow teammates was exciting enough, even without all the rest of it.

There was not only excitement, but a certain tension in the air. Not out on the surface where you could see it clearly, but hidden so that you might not notice it if you didn't look closely. It was great fun to laugh at each other falling off the water skis, or to wrestle on Whittaker's lawn, or to sit around at night talking about mountains and narrow escapes and favorite climbs. But at the same time each man was looking the others over very carefully, and his mind was full of questions (which he never told to anyone else): Am I good enough to be on this team? Am I one of the better climbers here, or am I one of the worse? Is there anyone here who thinks like I do, and has the same ideas about things? Who is going to be my best friend, and who is going to irritate me? The biggest questions were about climbing: How strong am I compared to these others? Will I be able to endure as much as the next man? Is there anyone who wants to climb Mt. Everest more than I do?

One of the big reasons we were here was for each man to decide what kind of team he was on and begin to take his place on it. We had to begin to grow together into a <u>team</u> and not just a group, and the first step was to get these first questions out of the way.

I feel sure that I was far more conscious of such questions than almost anyone else. I had no more experience with mountains than you do—possibly less—and I don't mind saying that I was very unsure of how I would do. The others had all tried themselves in many mountain situations and had at least a general idea of how they took to discomfort, how much will-power they had to keep going when they didn't want to go on, how their spirits held up under hardship. It's true that you can't possibly know for sure what a mountain like Everest is going to do to you, what demands it might make on every part of your nature; but no one on the team had less to go on than I in judging his own future performance. I felt more than a little anxious about it, but at the same time overjoyed and exhilarated. After all, this is the real meaning of Adventure: to risk something unknown, unpredictable, to welcome the New because it gives a chance for you to learn something you didn't already know. If you were to read many books about mountaineering and exploring of all kinds, you would find the adventurers talking a great deal about not only what they learned of the world—about the North Pole, lost cities in Peru, or the bottom of the sea—but also what they learned of themselves. Well, I was a little tired of my world and of my self, and I was ready to learn something new about both!

Mt. Rainier is about 80 miles from Seattle by car. We drove to it on our third day there, and I was in an old pick-up truck with Jerstad. He talked to me about things that had happened to him during his many guiding trips up and down Rainier, about the dangerous places where rocks are continually falling after breaking off higher up, about a time when he spent two weeks living on the summit, and about the pleasures he got from guiding people who enjoyed themselves in the mountains. He talked to me about some of the other team members; I learned for example that Barry Bishop (the Barrel) had been suspicious about having a "head-shrinker"—a term some people use for psychologists like me—along on a mountaineering expedition, but that he had decided maybe I would be all right, and I wondered whether any of the others had made up their minds yet. Most of all I got a good sense of Jerstad's own tremendous energy and drive, and his cheerfulness. He wanted badly to get to the top of our mountain. He seemed to have a deep well of confidence in himself, but it was combined with humility and a genuine respect for the surprises the future always holds.

We spent the night at Paradise Cove, and went to bed early after seeing two movies about the Himalayas that Dyhrenfurth had made several years earlier. The effect of seeing the movies, which began to bring home the beauty of Nepal and the almost overwhelming size and majesty of its mountains, was powerful. I'm sure I had all kinds of dreams that night about what might be coming, but in the morning they were gone. I woke with only a pleasant sense of great experiences lying ahead of me (something I hadn't felt for years), and some concern about my first attempt to keep up with America's best mountaineers on our climb to 10,000 feet on Rainier planned for that day.

The climb was rocky and tiring at first, but eventually brought us onto wide snow-fields, the lower ends of the many glaciers on Rainier. From there on to Camp Muir it was just a matter of putting one foot in front of the other, with each step moving higher. The important thing, I learned, is to find a pace slow enough that you can keep it steady, absolutely steady; once you find that pace, you can keep going even though you are very tired. No point in speeding up when someone passes you, or in stopping for a long refreshing rest, or in changing your pace as your thoughts speed up or slow down. I did all of these things, of course. And I was further distracted by the beauty of the view, which got more glorious with almost each step, once we were on the snow. As the sun was about to go down, I finally reached camp. Everyone else was there (except for Jim Ullman who was held down to my speed by a bad leg), and there was much joking about my being able to reach camp at all, which I heartily agreed was a miracle.

The first night on that ridge of rock and snow, and during the next day of skirting along the edge of deep crevasses (deep, open cracks), climbing in and out of them on ropes and small wire ladders, and calling on my body for more energy than I had asked it for in years, I had very strongly the feeling that perhaps I had made a terrible mistake. Perhaps I shouldn't have gotten into this at all! These men were so much at home up here, they belonged here more than they did on a street in town in city clothes. The air was filled with talk of mountain memories, of equipment, of how much danger one ought to risk and still be called sensible—all in all I felt as if I had gotten on a train for Miami, and then found out it was going to Siberia.

But I never had that feeling again, after that first day on Rainier, not even after Breitenbach had been killed in the icefall of the Khumbu Glacier and I had to decide whether going through the icefall was a risk I wanted to take. (It took me a week to decide, but I never wished I didn't have to make the decision.) As the group began to become a team, I felt that I had fallen in with a remarkable crew and that the chance to go to the world's highest mountains in their company was one of the rarest privileges likely to come my way in a life-time. And now that it is over, I'm even more sure that is true.

THE GRAND TOUR

After the Rainier session there were still five months to wait. Everyone went home to make things ready for the trip, to see that his family and affairs were taken care of while he was gone, and to do a certain amount of physical conditioning.

Big Jim did a lot of water-skiing and worked out with weights, and the effect was obvious. Jake and Barry Corbet were running through the valleys and woods of Jackson, Wyoming, and getting out for several good rock climbs every week. Dick Emerson, in Cincinnati, didn't have much chance to get into hills or woods but would go up and down four flights of stairs, with his eighty-pound eight-year-old son on his back, for half an hour every afternoon. Dan Doody was racing motorists around Los Angeles on his Schwinn bicycle, while Norman was playing a lot of tennis and doing push-ups on his fingertips.

I was living in Berkeley, California, near to both Gil Roberts and Will Siri. Some evenings Gil and I went together to the local high school track, and I would run a series of quarter-miles while he ran a series of miles. Later, when I had worked up to running miles myself, I began going out on the streets in the very early morning, running up and down the hills of Berkeley, frightening old men—out walking because they couldn't sleep—when I burst out of the fog behind them. Later still, as my endurance built up, I often went out for long runs with Will, over the unpopulated hills east of Berkeley. He was like a tightly coiled spring, and although he was ten years older than I, he could always outdistance me. When we got out among the trees, the sober, soft-spoken scientist changed into a forest sprite, nimble, young again, running hard at a tree and planting both feet firmly against the side of it, propelling himself into the air again as if he were on a string. It was clear that there was a child hidden inside of Will, who came out only when he was out of his office, away from his home, alone with himself and Nature. I often wondered what that child thought about when Siri was in his laboratory in his white coat, poring over reports—or when he was laying down the law to his own to children.

I hope I will never forget the delicious excitement that built up as February 3rd came closer. Christmas and New Year meant almost nothing to me that year; I had no wife and children at the time, and I was almost completely occupied with reading the accounts of other expeditions, studying pictures of Nepal, of Everest and of some of the other Titans in that part of the world: Kangchenjunga (third highest in the world), Makalu, Cho Oyu, Ama Dablam. How little power even the best picture has to make you know what it will feel like to see such mountains with your own eyes, to be there! But they were better than nothing, and I had no mind for anything else.

Time moved like molasses, but inevitably we arrived at February 2nd, and all the team members (except for Norman, Dan, and the Barrel, who had gone over a month earlier, and Unsoeld, who was already in Nepal working for the Peace Corps) arrived in San Francisco.

Jim Lester leaving for Everest via a tour of Asia, February 3, 1963

Look at a globe showing the earth. Find San Francisco on the west coast of America. Then with your finger move out into the Pacific Ocean and as you go turn partly to the south. This is what we did, on the first leg of a very long flight in a Pan American Boeing 707 jet. We stopped first in Honolulu, though only for an hour. The next stop was to be Tokyo, Japan, which you will find if you continue on over the rest of the Pacific after Hawaii. But we had strong winds against us, and the pilot decided we had to make a stop on the way, for more fuel. Look again at the globe: there aren't many places to stop out there! We had to go south again, and find a tiny island just big enough for a jet landing strip: Wake Island, which both the U.S. Navy and Pan American use for stop-overs like these. We landed in Tokyo after fifteen hours of flying, in the fastest plane you can buy a ticket on.

Tokyo was our entrance to Asia, and once we were in Japan we all began to forget a little our excitement about going to Everest. We became absorbed in the colors, the smells, the sounds, the new kinds of faces—even the ways people moved seemed different. We were not only going to the highest mountain in the world, we were on a Grand Tour of Asia, and we stopped in some of the major cities there: Hong Kong, which is on an island just a mile off the coast of Communist China; then Bangkok, capital of Thailand; then Calcutta, India, a city where we saw so many poor people that some of the men didn't have the heart even to take their pictures.

Boy getting haircut, Hong Kong

In Calcutta, we went into a huge bazaar, where you could buy almost anything under the sun, to look for hats—hats to shade our eyes and keep our brains from boiling in the hot Nepalese sun during the three-week approach march, and on the return march. It was easy to get separated in the bazaar, and almost impossible to find your way. But we had no trouble because swarms of children took an interest in us, and whenever two or three of us seemed to be lost they would take us by the sleeve, with much chattering and laughing, and lead us back to the rest of the group. By the time we had found a hat stall, word had gotten around the bazaar about us. We could hardly move because of all the people who crowded around wanting to show us hats, try them on us, run somewhere and get different sizes if these wouldn't fit (no matter what numbers were printed inside the hats, there seemed to be only two sizes: too big and too small!). When it was all over and the dust settled, I couldn't see how anyone knew how many hats they had sold us, or whether anyone had paid. It seemed that the actual business didn't matter—they were just glad for some relief from the boredom of sitting around with so little to do!

Some time later, after several weeks at Advance Base Camp (21,300 feet) with almost nothing to do, I felt the same way. The smallest event—say, a Gorak (a large black bird like a raven) wandering into camp to scrounge some food—became an occasion, and something to talk about over dinner. It's funny to think what a newspaper about our life on Everest might have looked like. In the city people won't stop and buy a paper unless there are headlines such as:

ASTRONAUT WALKS IN SPACE!!!

or

17-CAR PILE-UP ON FREEWAY!!!

But at Advance Base Camp it would have been enough if the headlines had read only:

GORAK WANDERS INTO CAMP!!!

or

BEAR SLEEPS THROUGH BREAKFAST!!!

That last one would <u>really</u> have been news, because there were two things the Bear loved above all else: sleeping and eating. But he never let the one interfere with the other.

———

Until Calcutta, we had been flying in big jets. Now we were to fly into a very small country, Nepal, where there are no landing places for jets and not enough passengers going in and out to fill such jets. We boarded, instead, a rather elderly DC-3, run by the Royal Nepalese Airlines. The airline is very small, and run in such a casual friendly way that, for example, when Dave Dingman told the pilot that he too had a pilot's license, the pilot turned the plane over to him, so that he could go back and have a smoke with the passengers!

The only other passenger I remember was a Buddhist monk in a beautiful orange robe, but there must have been a few other ones besides us.

It was a thrilling flight, more so even than our flights over the Pacific and between the cities where we stopped. Leaving Calcutta, the land was very flat, like Illinois or Kansas. As we flew into Nepal we began to cross soft hills, like rolling waves in the earth's crust. These became small mountains, rounded and covered with trees. It was a crystal-clear day, and we could see to the horizon, probably 100 miles away. We were all quiet with the knowledge that the Grand Tour was over, and that we were about to put hotels, bathtubs, restaurants, busy streets, electric lights, radios, airplanes—all the business of civilized life—behind us, and start living a life in which everyone would be much more on his own. And most of us were longing for this, longing above all for the challenge of high, snowy mountains. We were feeling near now to those magical, unreachable places: the Himalayas, and incredibly, Mt. Everest.

I don't know who saw it first, out of the window of the plane. Someone shouted, "There it is!" and everyone rushed to the right side of the plane, straining to see past a lot of noses to the white jagged line of peaks that stretched all along the horizon. There were so many summits, so far away! In spite of all the pictures I had studied I couldn't be sure which mountain was Everest; none had shown this view, and besides, whichever it was, it was so distant that you could barely make out any definite shapes. From 100 miles away you couldn't tell which was the highest mountain; the whole range looked staggeringly big.

But once pointed out it was clear which it was. Everest—and

only one other peak on the whole horizon—had a plume of clouds forming behind it, like a flag on a flag-pole. We stared, we shouted, we clapped each other on the back, we took rolls of film with different exposures and different lenses, we ran back and forth the length of the plane looking for the best window to shoot through—I think the noise and excitement were even greater than when the summit was actually reached three months later!

It reminds me now of a big football game. The crowds jostle each other into the stadium, find their seats, look around to see their friends, and finally settle down to wait for something to appear on the now-empty green field—and suddenly one of the two teams runs out onto the field, the band strikes up a march, cheerleaders jump up and down, and everyone feels a big, tingly "now-something's-going-to-happen" feeling.

Everest had appeared on the field, and as we were the other team, it was our turn next.

KATHMANDU

There is no city in America or Europe to compare with Kathmandu. It doesn't sparkle, it doesn't glitter, it certainly isn't boring but it doesn't make your heart pound faster either. It simply surrounds you with an atmosphere like a fairy-tale.

For Westerners, it is so much like a dream itself that makes a perfect place for beginning a march to a mountain you have so far known only in dreams.

Kathmandu suspends you exactly between familiar everyday "real" things and places—like houses, streets, policemen, knives and forks, or earth—and another kind of world; unfamiliar, mysterious, unreal, a world of pure imagination, where anything can happen and nothing is really what it seems to be.

We stayed a week in Kathmandu, working to get the 29 tons (58,000 pounds) of supplies ready for the backs of the porters, and resting several days by roaming this strange town on foot and on bicycle. Everything I saw fascinated me. Several times I got up at 5:30 or 6 a.m. to take a walk or a run in the early morning mist—as I did in Berkeley, but how different! The people on the street—including an ancient and tiny street-sweeping woman—paid me almost no attention, even though I was a kind of giant at 195 pounds, rumbling along the sidewalk in my peculiar clothes. She apparently believed, as I came to, that almost anything could happen in Kathmandu.

Loads being packed for the backs of 907 porters

Captain James "Jimmy" Roberts overseeing supplies and transport

A ration of Kentucky bourbon being weighed

But what I remember the most clearly about the town are two short moments of listening to music. They both occurred on one evening when I was out walking with Emerson, looking into the very dimly lit little shops hardly big enough for a man to stand up straight in, making detours around sacred Hindu cows sleeping in the middle of the dusty streets.

We were drawn to one building by loud singing, great cymbal clashing and I don't know what other kinds of more or less musical sounds. It was coming from the second story, not very high, and apparently had no beginning or end. It may have been a card party that was turning into a slightly drunken brawl, or it may have been some kind of religious ceremony—it was impossible for me to judge. Something about the singing almost hypnotized me, and I felt the whole atmosphere of the city concentrated in that one spot. We made some tape-recordings there, and then moved on into the darkness of a small street at the end of which there was a little light and possibly some activity. There, in a little roofed-over patio beside a house, by candle-light, five old men were playing instruments I'm not even sure I could recognize, making a strange but wonderful sound in the warm night air. Again, it may have been religious music—or it may have been something like a jazz-session, with each man making up his part as he went. There were a few people in the streets listening but no one seemed to notice Dick and me. Time seemed to have stopped completely. It was as if the whole scene were a painting.

We stayed until we remembered that on the next day we were starting the 185-mile walk into Everest country, and decided we should get some rest.

EAST TOWARD EVEREST

At first glance it seems unfortunate that to get from Kathmandu to the foot of Everest requires a hike of about 185 miles. But it isn't unfortunate, first because it is one of the most interesting hikes a person could ever find, and second because it builds muscles and helps you get slowly used to greater and greater altitude.

The reason such a long hike is required is that there is no need for roads in most of Nepal, as outside of Kathmandu there is almost nothing but tiny farms and no one can afford cars or trucks. There is trade among the villages, and back in the hills the Sherpas have always traded with Tibet. But <u>all</u> of this trade is done on foot, even though some of the loads that porters have to carry from one place, for sale in another, weigh up to 150 pounds. The country is covered by a network of footpaths, and these combined with many strong legs form the transportation system of Nepal.

Another reason there are no roads on which wheels could travel between Kathmandu and the Solo Khumbu Valley, at the foot of Everest, is the nature of the country. East toward Everest you move immediately into the foothills of the Himalaya. These foothills gradually grow toward the size of the American Rockies (up to around 12,000 feet), and then you are ready to enter the land of the mountains themselves, the true Himalayas. In country like this, building even a small highway would be an enormous task, requiring huge amounts of labor (and machines, which Nepal does not have) and of money. It simply is not worth it to anyone, yet, to invest in these costs.

Our first job, then, was to get ourselves and all our supplies over these footpaths. It seems hard, even for me now, to picture how we could have had so much weight to carry. But once we left Kathmandu we had to live entirely on what we could bring with us. The local food and water were safe enough for the Nepalese to eat and drink, but contained tiny organisms that could make foreigners unused to them violently and sometimes incurably ill. (Naturally we didn't carry our own water. We drank what we could find, away from villages, but only after filtering out the majority of such organisms and then dropping pills in it to kill the rest.)

As for clothing, we needed a considerable variety. We needed cool things, like shorts and lightweight shirts, for the early part of the approach, when the weather was warm and sometimes very hot, and the trail required so much knee-bending that long pants would have been a nuisance.

Drying socks and boots, approach march

Later on, at greater altitudes, it would be colder, requiring heavier underclothes and some outer garments to protect us from wind and rain or snow on the trail. And finally, as we came into the region around Everest, we would change into actual mountaineering clothes. All of this, and several changes of each kind of clothing, for us and also for the Sherpas, had to be brought with us. And there was also heavy equipment that would make life and climbing possible once we had reached our base camp: fifty-two tents, three kinds of special boots, hundreds of little butane-gas stoves (as there is no wood on the Khumbu Glacier!), coils and coils of rope for tying one climber to another, metal pitons for securing rope to rock, crampons for helping us to walk on snow and ice, extra ice-axes, oxygen tanks for the highest camps, and so on, for a long list.

Not twenty Americans—not even twenty Sherpas—can carry 29 tons across the street, much less over the approach to Everest. For this, we hired 907 porters—people who lived out from Kathmandu in the valleys and hills, whose backs and legs are used to struggling up and down steep hills on rocky trails with a bulky load on the back. For about 75 cents a day per porter we got reliable men, women, and even some children to carry boxes of between 50 and 65 pounds. And to manage and supervise these porters, 32 of our 37 high-altitude Sherpas made the trip down from their homes around Namche Bazar, close to Everest. When we finally got under way, then, on February 20th, 1963, we were 19 (Jim Ullman rode out on horseback to our first night's camp, but returned the next day to Kathmandu) plus 32 Sherpas plus 907 porters—a total of 958 persons, plus at least 50 more relatives of porters, since a number of whole families traveled together even though only one member might be acting as porter.

What one human can dream of, behind his eyes, it may take a thousand to realize. We were now more like an army moving heavily toward the front lines than we were like an eager football team rushing out to meet the opposition.

Porters and high-altitude Sherpas, the latter distinguished by their red hats and expedition gear

---

I will never forget the hour of taking the first steps. The porters were being assigned their loads, in a very orderly fashion, and we were milling among these men and women with whom we were now going to spend several weeks in close quarters. We tried to get the feeling of what kind of people they were, and wondered what they thought of us and our project. Finally at about 11 in the morning, along with the first porters who had fitted their boxes comfortably on their backs, hanging most of the weight from a "tump-line" which ran over the top of their head and under the bottom of the box, we casually strolled away from the scene, on the trail to Panchkhal, the first night's stop. Inside my head I heard a trumpet fanfare, and cheers from all the friends and relatives I knew were wishing me well on this trip. I felt the first steps ought to be a little dance, to celebrate what was happening here, but they were only plodding ones, merely the first of many, many, many.

But the approach march was not boring—far from it. Once the first blisters had hardened over, and you found your pace and the weight of the pack you wanted to carry, you were free then to take in the people and places around you. No two days of countryside were quite the same. Some hours we were pushing and panting to reach the ridge of a steep hillside (and on these trails there had been no attempt to make the journey <u>easy</u>, but only to make it reach the village at the other end in as short a time as possible, which often meant going straight up extremely steep inclines), other hours we were descending the equally steep far side of the hill, or moving along the bank of a stream, and then starting up the next hill. No two villages looked exactly alike; the style of building houses changed as we moved along, and there were distinct differences between the faces seen along the trail.

Everything was new and held interest for us. This is one of the great pleasures of such an expedition. People get in the habit of going about their daily business, hardly noticing anything around them, taking it all for granted because they see it every day—if one can call that seeing. It's only when you take yourself out of your everyday surroundings—or at least out of your everyday way of looking at things—that you really see much detail or really notice how interesting <u>things</u> can be. To see freshly this way, to find pleasure in the color of some wall you pass, or to notice how all the angles of things fit together as you look down a path through a village, to notice how your mood changes depending on how far you can see, all this is intensely <u>refreshing</u> in a strange way. Some people call it seeing again as a child sees, as if for the first time, and I was very interested to notice that on the approach march many of us (myself included) had dreams of our own childhoods, of seeing people and places that we hadn't seen or thought of since we were perhaps 12 or 13, especially of old forgotten girl-friends! Also, most of us began having many more dreams in color than we are used to having at home. Just as our surroundings seemed more vivid to us, so did our dreams.

Even though we were often very tired, often hot and almost always sweaty and dirty, even though there were too many people on these narrow trails and if you got caught in among them you could get bumped around uncomfortably, and your feet or your knees or your shoulders often hurt from the strain being put on them—in spite of all this, it was still refreshing. Away from habits and routines and schedules, life came alive again—just as it used to for me when school was out and I went away to summer camp.

———

The day on the trail usually started about 6 a.m., with a sleepy half-awakening to the noise of porters talking animatedly around their breakfast fires or searching out their assigned loads and moving out of camp. Each two Americans had one Sherpa assigned to them, whose job in the morning was to take down their Sahibs' tent, gather up their personal belongings, and have their packs ready for them after breakfast. Our Sherpa would appear and urge us out of our sleeping bags so that they could drop it and turn it over to its porter, and we were forced out into the chilly dawn air to pull on socks and boots, shorts and shirt, and try to stay warm until the sun rose higher in the sky.

Expedition-issue tent, expedition-issue underwear

Breakfast might be grapefruit juice, bread or crackers and jelly, and some hot chocolate, obtained in a general free-for-all from a small table. The big thing was to dress, eat, and get going ahead of the bulk of the porters, because if you failed to get going in time—if you took too long to prepare the coverings on your blisters, or couldn't find your Sherpa and your pack, or if you just plain slept too late—you were likely to be trapped all day in the middle of a crowd of pushing and pulling, shouting and laughing, sweating and spitting, porters who care little for

The mess tent

what plans <u>you</u> might have on the trail, who as often as not only laughed at the poor climber trying to force his way through a sea of boxes-with-legs or around the outside of two porters stopped to rest in the middle of the path. More than once I got the corner of a box in the ribs just as I was about to pass someone, and wondered how accidental it was.

Out ahead of the mob, the trail belonged entirely to the one who was treading it. I often walked for hours seeing no one except maybe a teammate stopped for some water or to take a picture, or a small child watching me from behind a stone wall. It was a funny feeling, for hours, days, weeks, never knowing what one might find around the next bend or over the next hill. I started almost every new day with a light-hearted feeling, not so much because I knew that by dark we would be 10 or 12 miles closer to Chomolungma but just from looking forward to the pleasures of the day along the trail. Even though I often arrived in camp in a condition that would have to be considered pitiful, the memories of painful hours faded quickly and I usually woke up eager for what the new day might show me.

We usually stopped beside the trail around 10 a.m., for a lunch which usually consisted of more juice, cereal and powdered milk, bread and cheese, hot coffee, and maybe some dried prunes or a chocolate bar for dessert. Besides providing nourishment, these stops were welcomed for the chance to stop under some trees or by a stream, to stretch out on your back and to air hot feet, to compare notes with teammates about what we had been thinking of along the trail. Sometimes we got into heated "discussions" about subjects such as religion or politics or science, but more often the subject would be something like whether it is wiser to drive a Volkswagen or a Corvette. The two doctors, Gil Roberts and Dave Dingman, sometimes could be heard discussing patients or the kind of medical work they wanted to do some day. Big Jim might talk about his sons, or how his store back in Seattle was doing without him. Missing my record collection, I often liked to talk about music.

The evening's camp was usually reached, by the Sherpas who went ahead to set it up, around 2 or 3 in the afternoon, and the climbers filtered in between perhaps 2 and 4. This may seem like stopping a little early in the day, when we could have made another two or three miles by continuing until sundown. But don't forget that we were an army, not a patrol. If camp were set up by 3 p.m., the porters (who as a rule were strung out over several miles during the day) would be streaming in until 6 or 7 p.m. Camp had to be established early enough so that the last porters could arrive before sundown, to stake out a sleeping area and find firewood while there was still light.

Porters settling for the evening

Most evenings, after dinner, we sat around a gaslight and wrote letters or talked quietly with each other. Bedtime was early, and even if one read in the tent for a while we were usually asleep by 9. On two evenings, though, our Sherpas, glad to be getting back up into the hills and closer to their homes, broke out in song and dance, and their spirits were not dampened by our coming to watch. I'm very fond of my memory of one scene in particular: ten or eleven of our strongest high-altitude porters, strong little men who two months later would be carrying loads up through the snow at 24, 25, 26,000 feet, sometimes without oxygen—ten or eleven of these little men in a line, arms around each others' shoulders, doing a lazy, delicate little dance step together, in the red light of several small fires, ringed by an audience of 70 or 80 porter men and women, quietly enjoying it. Coming as it did after some group singing of ours (such things as "You Are My Sunshine") which was noisy and out of tune and pretty poor, really—I felt the Sherpa performance was a true work of art.

Behind all this variety and color and change, there was one big fact: we <u>were</u> getting closer and closer to Mt. Everest. The rigors of the trail would have seemed more like hardships if there had not been something worthwhile at the other end of that trail.

For fifteen days we made our way up and down foothills, through forests, and along rivers, and we seldom got a glimpse of the really high mountains. We hadn't seen Everest since that brief hour in the DC-3, and it began to seem that we were never going to reach it, that we had gotten started on a hike that would never end. But the sixteenth day was an occasion, and a time for celebrating, because we reached Namche Bazar, 12,200 feet high, home of many of our Sherpas, a tiny village on a steep hillside made famous by the books in which mountaineers have talked about it. My diary for that day, March 7th, says:

> Awoke to a clear, beautiful day though expecting rain. Surrounded by high rock walls and a view of ice and snow mountains. A gentle up and down traverse along the Dudh Kosi (a river), crossing it at least twice. More and more views of really high mountains. Perfectly gorgeous and magnificent country, to the lunch stop. Left lunch stop with the first ones, Pownall and Corbet. A steep climb (3000 feet?) with a view first of Nuptse ridge, later Everest through the clouds. Almost cried at first view of Everest. Continued climbing steeply, until Dawa Tenzing (my Sherpa) gave

me a cup of <u>chang</u> (a kind of wine or beer made from rice) which he had brought down from his house in Namche. On from there, almost alone with Pownall, Corbet, Sherpa Ang Norbu. Arrived in Namche, led by sentries to a chang-house, where Noddy and check-point officer had arranged a reception more or less. Two girls of 14 or 15 kept our glasses full . . . Tremendous feeling of <u>having arrived</u> . . .

The view from Namche Bazar

I think that at that point I had much the same feelings of elation and success that the more experienced climbers, whose goals were higher, had when they reached the summit of Everest.

I drank enough chang so that I don't remember the rest of that afternoon very well. Vaguely I remember wrestling with Hornbein on the grass, and then later Hornbein and Emerson and I helping each other up the hillside to our tents above the village. I think we must have slept for a while. The fog came in swiftly and damply late in the afternoon, so that we had to eat inside two of our larger tents. That night, Pasang Phutar, our chief Sherpa, gave a big party at his house, the largest in town. There was food and drink that was hard to get down, and there was a great deal of singing and dancing.

What a contrast with life on the trail up to now! At this moment and in this place we were having the best of two worlds: we were back where humans live together, in houses, eating off tables, and providing warmth for each other. And we were also close enough to Everest—a place that could hardly have less to do with human life—almost to taste it!

THE FINAL APPROACH

From Namche to Base Camp was only about 20 miles—for Goraks. For those who had to walk it rather than fly, who couldn't follow a straight line over the towering mountain ridges and peaks on the way and had to detour around them, it was more like 40 miles. Covering the distance took four more camps, the fifth being Base.

The first stop after Namche was to be an ancient Buddhist monastery called Thyangboche. It is set on top of a ridge at about 12,300 feet, and both ends of the ridge curve upward like an old overworked horse's back, becoming peaks of over 20,000 feet. In this setting the white and brown buildings of the monastery seemed as small as a few leaves on the ground among huge redwood trees. Yet in fact the ridge was as wide as a football field and there was a nice feeling of room to move around in there.

I left Namche with Jake, just the two of us somewhat ahead of the rest. The trail curved gently around the hillside, descending gradually to the Dudh Kosi river and going through a pleasant wooded section on the way. It was snowing very lightly as we went along, without speaking, and among the trees I saw many scenes that reminded me of postcard pictures of New England. There was a homey, almost cozy feeling here, and I forgot that beyond our next stop there would be no more human life except our own—no more villages, kitchen fires, children playing on the grass, dogs barking. Beyond Thyangboche in the winter nothing happened except snowfall, drifting clouds, the cracking of ice as the long Khumbu Glacier moved down from Lhotse under the pressure of its own unimaginable weight. Like all the others before us, we were pushing life into a place where life did not occur naturally, depending on our planning, ingenuity, endurance, and good luck to see us through.

Jake and I rested at the river for a while and were joined by Dan Doody, who had not been feeling well for several days, because of the altitude. Weakness, headaches, and sometimes nausea were the usual symptoms of "altitude-sickness" and he had them all. Jake went ahead with some others, and Dan and I finished the long, zigzag climb up the hillside very, very slowly, with the snow coming down harder all the time. By the time we reached the camp on the ridge, it was practically a blizzard.

Bad weather kept us on the monastery grounds for five days, three or four more than we had planned to stay. Climbers and Sherpas could have moved on through the snow, but the problem was the porters, some of whom were still going along the trail in their bare feet. Without the porters and our supplies there was no point in pushing forward, so we accepted Thyangboche as home for a while, and I have never seen a more beautiful place for a home. We used the time to distribute climbing equipment, to take hikes up the steep hillsides to help us get used to the altitude, to write letters, read, play bridge, build snowmen, and visit with the monks who lived all year round in this superb spot.

The camp at Thyangboche

The monastery was an eerie, fascinating place, very dark inside but painted in striking red and gold, with heavy purple cloth hanging in the doorways instead of doors because it does a better job of barring the wind and holding the heat in. In the main prayer-room we saw eight monks sitting on rugs on the floor, four across from four, chanting softly as they read from hand-written scrolls of parchment. Every so often one on the end would turn to his side and strike a large brass gong, sending a thick rumble, yet sharp around the edges, through the room; at other times several would pick up long horns lying beside them and blow them gently to produce low, wavering, peculiar sounds. Little men, in a dark room, lost on the edge of the Himalaya, doing honor to their gods, praying for Buddha-knows-what. A strange, strange atmosphere, but much more suitable to where we were than, say, a Methodist sermon.

On March 15, our sixth morning in Thyangboche and our twenty-fourth day out from Kathmandu, Norman decided that we must move on regardless. We had a schedule for climbing and deadlines to meet, and to get too far behind schedule might spoil our whole chance of putting anyone on the summit. And so with the temperature at about 20° F, with four to eight inches of snow on the trail, we broke camp and began the final approach to Everest.

Getting to Pheriche, a summer yak-herding plateau at about 14,000 feet, was a matter of going down from Thyangboche to the Dudh Kosi still once more, then a long hill climb and finally an easy path along the hillside curving slowly into the valley of Pheriche. The next day brought a long haul that I found extremely hard, up the hills at the far end of the valley, on to the tip end of the Khumbu Glacier (which reached all the way to here), up, up—I felt the footsteps that I was following in the snow would never level out, and yet I was running out of strength. I wondered if they would have to carry me to Base Camp! It did my morale good to see that some of the other, stronger, men were also having trouble. Doody was still feeling terrible and had a very unhappy look on his face as he slogged along. I saw Al Auten drop beside the trail for a while, unable to go on. Even the Bear admitted wondering where his strength had gone.

The answer was that we had reached an altitude (about 15,000 feet at the lunch stop) at which serious new demands are put on the body and which requires it to shift gears. Using more gas in the old gear could get us to Namche and Thyangboche in pretty fair shape, but to go higher our bodies would have to make some more radical adjustments. The climb this day found many of us between gears, and without much push. For no reason that I understand, others were not affected on this day: Hornbein and Unsoeld, Whittaker and Jerstad, steamed ahead as if they were at sea level.

I remember dragging myself into the camp at Lobuje (16,200 feet), drinking a quart and a half of lemonade almost without stopping, having my first meal since breakfast the day before (I had been quite sick since our meal with the monks), and sitting exhausted in the open until dinner at 6 and bed at 7:15. What bliss it was to climb deep down inside a heavy sleeping bag, warm as toast though the temperature outside was now going to 2° F at night, to run over the scenes and events of the day in comfort, making the difficulties seem so minor compared to how they seemed when they were happening!

We weren't sure whether or not another camp would be required between Lobuje and Base Camp; it depended on the condition of the glacier and how hard the going might be. On the 18th of March a patrol went out to study the situation, returning at the end of the day very tired and of the opinion that we should indeed set up one more stop before Base. They had picked the place, a desolate spot on the frozen lake between two sloping hills, the same place which had been used as a base camp by the Swiss team eight years before us. We moved from Lobuje to this lake camp (or Gorakshep as the Sherpas called it, meaning "burial place of the Goraks"; maybe this is where the old birds go, like elephants, to die) in small groups, on different days, according to how rested we felt and how ready to take the higher altitude (17,000 feet).

As soon as everyone was into Gorakshep, the advance party—Norman, Will Siri, Lute, Big Jim, and Willi Unsoeld, along with 23 Sherpas—forged ahead over the glacier surface to find a spot for Base Camp. Phantom Alley, they called the route they covered, because here the ice has cracked into crevasses, risen up into hills, and most dramatically of all has pushed up pinnacles to as much as thirty feet, cresting a maze so complicated that if clouds had hid the world's highest peaks by which we were steering ourselves, it would have been almost impossible to find our way. It was the kind of place that fascinates and gets a hold on you. You stop thinking about hours or days, and start thinking about eternity because your surroundings seem so utterly timeless, without beginning or end, like the music in Kathmandu. Divers beneath the sea often know this kind of fascination, and sometimes don't want to come up again. I have heard people say they know of sport parachute-jumpers who died, not because their parachute failed to work, but because the jumper became fascinated with the experience of falling and didn't want to end it by pulling the rip-cord. The first astronaut to "take a walk" in space is reported to have stayed outside his space capsule eight minutes longer than he was supposed to have done; he too seems to have felt this uncanny sense of being "out of this world" and reluctant to come back.

Porter navigating Phantom Alley

But the sight of Everest, now looming almost directly above us, looking so <u>attainable</u> to my unpracticed eye, was too compelling for anyone to be distracted from it. Everyone passed through Phantom Alley and moved into his quarters at Base Camp: a tent shared with one other person, perched on snow, the snow lying on top of a jumble of huge boulders, the boulders lying on top of a thick river of ice, the Khumbu Glacier.

Base Camp and the Khumbu icefall

Here we were, as Jim Ullman later wrote, "earth's highest community". The population was 72 once the bulk of the porters had dumped their loads and left. Our little community included the expedition members, now numbering 19; Captain "Noddy" Rana, our government-assigned Nepalese liaison officer; our 32 original Sherpas plus five additional "high" Sherpas; 12 "semi-high" porters hired from the others to offer extra help in the icefall; and three kitchen helpers for our cook.

We had two large tents here used as living and reading rooms except at meal times, when they became (without changing) dining rooms. The Sherpas had set up a kitchen and store-room arrangement, made out of rocks and boxes and tarpaulins, about 50 yards away from the main tents, in which they prepared our food and theirs. Such "luxury" led the San Francisco Chronicle to call us "Pampered Americans on Everest", but we were grateful for such pampering. We would not have eaten so well if, after a hard climb or a return from a higher camp, we had

Base Camp meal supplies and possibly a helper to the cook, Danu

had to prepare our own food. And since appetite becomes a problem at these altitudes and eating is so important to keep strength up, I should think this seeming luxury was more of a necessity. We even had a bathroom tent at Base Camp! But most of us found that the trouble required to unzip the tent, climb in, undo several layers of heaving clothing in a tiny space, redo them, climb out and zip it again, was hardly worth the protection from the wind. Besides, speaking for myself, I hated to cut myself off from our spectacular views just for the sake of making "going to the bathroom" more like home. In any case, no one froze his bottom, despite repeated exposure here and much higher up!

Base Camp was really a very comfortable place, considering where we were. Almost two months later I found myself feeling almost as reluctant to leave it as I have felt about leaving every other place I have lived and loved.

The view from Lester's tent, Base Camp

CONQUEST OF CHAOS

Base Camp was located at almost 18,000 feet, just at a point where the Khumbu Glacier makes a sharp left turn in its almost imperceptible descent. Below Base, the wide band of ice ran fairly smoothly (except for Phantom Alley) down in the direction of Pheriche. Above Base the picture was quite different. The glacier reached down to Base from 2000 feet above, at a steep decline, and in this drop it acted much like a waterfall, churning, tumbling over itself, changing shape more often and more quickly than the main body of the glacier above and below it. All of this went on at an extremely slow rate, of course, compared to water. It was as if you looked at water photographed in very, very slow-motion. So slow, in fact, that unless you <u>knew</u> it to be so, you couldn't be sure that all the groaning, creaking, cracking, booming activity was really part of a steady snail-like movement downhill of the ice. This steeply descending section of the glacier is called the icefall, and within it small avalanches occurred daily, crevasses were constantly opening up or closing, monstrous blocks of ice and snow were shifting and slipping, as the whole of the glacier moved downward. At the end of the day a map of the icefall would look quite different from the same map made in the morning.

No Western eyes—and possibly no eyes at all—had so much as seen this icefall before 1921, when two British climbers, [George Mallory, who died in an attempt to get to or from the summit in 1924, and Guy Bullock] tackling Everest from the Tibetan side, peered over the edge of the Lho La into the hollow where we were now camped. They could see at least the lower part of the Khumbu Icefall, could see that this might be another way to approach the summit but later wrote, "We have seen this Western glacier and are not sorry we have not to go up it. It is terribly steep and broken."

But since 1950, when Nepal first allowed foreigners to climb its mountains, there had been six teams of men who had studied the icefall and none of them had found ways to get through it. No one felt safe climbing among its towers and cliffs; Sir Edmund Hillary called it nothing but "tottering chaos," and when, at Thyangboche, I re-read descriptions written by the first men to see it from this close, I found myself doubting my own courage to face it. But from where we were there were only two ways to go: back to Kathmandu, or up through the icefall.

While most of us were still at Gorakshep, the first patrol left Base Camp to explore a route through the icefall. There was no obvious route to take, and to find one that was reasonably short and also reasonably safe (remember that there was absolutely no way to predict which part of the icefall might make the next move) was a job for the most skilled experts. Whittaker, Jerstad, and Unsoeld, with three Sherpas, spent most of March 22nd working their way upwards, planting little sticks with red flags on them to mark the route they slowly but surely were establishing. By 3:15 in the afternoon they had marked out a path more than half-way through it, better than any of them had thought they might do; they were able to get back down to Base before dark. There to meet them were Jake, the Barrel, Pownall, Gil, Dave, and Dan, all of whom had moved up to Base from Gorakshep that day.

Sherpa ready to plot a course through the icefall

On March 23rd, to give the first patrol a rest from their first exertions at such a high altitude (they had reached 19,300 feet), a second patrol went out to push the route even further into the icefall: Pownall, Sherpa Ang Pema, and Jake roped together into one three-man team; Gil and Sherpa Ila Tsering made a second team. They had a beautiful clear day in which to work, the air still and almost hot from all the reflected sunshine. Everything pointed toward easier going than we had expected. A hope began to grow, a hope that we might actually climb the mountain before May 1st and be back in

Kathmandu long before the appearance of the summer monsoons, which bring violent storms to the heights and rain, mud, and leeches to the foothills through which we would have to return. You could practically see optimism rising like a balloon above Base Camp. Until sometime during the afternoon.

I was at Gorakshep, doing nothing. The Bear was on a hill above camp. At about 3:30 he saw what looked like a large avalanche come off near the Lho La, which meant that there was some danger of its sweeping into—possibly over—Base Camp. He came down and suggested we should try to reach Base on our walkie-talkie, to make sure everything was all right. I tried but had no luck, and then Tom Hornbein took over and somehow made contact with Al, who reassured us—as far as we could get it through the crackling static—that the avalanche had hardly caught their attention, and that such things seemed to be commonplace there. However, he reported, there seemed to be something funny going on with the two teams in the icefall—with binoculars, he could only make out four men—and we should stand by for more news when they had figured out what was going on. Al was unable to reach the icefall party by walkie-talkie. He was clearly worried.

At 5 we managed to make contact again. There was news indeed. Jake was probably dead; no one knew for sure what had happened yet.

We had grown cocky about our mountain and were completely unprepared for this. Those of us at Gorakshep—including Barry Corbet, Jake's closest friend in the world—were simply stunned. We talked little to each other, stuffed something down for dinner, and asked ourselves silent stupid questions: Is it true? How could it happen? What's the meaning of it? What can we do now?

The next morning we moved as quickly as possible to join the rest of the team, to find out what had happened—that Jake had been crushed when a huge block of ice slipped onto him—and to do what we could.

Jake Breitenbach, far right, practicing rope skills with L-R Dick Emerson, an unidentifiable climber, Willi Unsoeld, Tom Hornbein, and Dave Dingman

---

It seems to me that in ordinary life, death always come as something unnatural, a sign that something has gone wrong. It is taken as an interruption of the normal, an intrusion into what people expect to happen, a dark stain on an otherwise lovely picture. It is something not to think about until it happens, and then to regret; it has no honorable place in the scheme of things.

For me at least, Jake's death was not like that. I said it was a shock and that we were stunned and not ready for it; that is true. But it didn't take long for most of us to accept Jake's removal from the scene. For one or two days it seemed terribly wrong, a miscalculation on someone's part; it wasn't proper that it should have happened. And then the accident took its place among the natural things of the world, and it no longer occurred to me to ask whether it was proper —just as I didn't ask whether it was proper that today should be cloudy and miserable when yesterday it was sunny and warm. It just was, and there was no hidden meaning to be found in it. Life is an unending stream of events and no one is sure of the meaning of any of them, really—this is as true of the things we desire as of those we do not desire, including death. I'm sure it was easier to reach this way of feeling about the fatal accident because of the way we were living—close to the earth, close to simple, basic things; we all felt we were closer than usual to the basically important things in life, and maybe that's why it was easier to accept death.

It may be, too, that our long hike through the foothills and our present location buried among such huge mountains helped. Compared to city life, our state of mind had shifted quietly away from considering human life the most important and outstanding thing in the world. We and the people around us were obviously a very small part of the picture in the Himalayas. Compared to the forces that had pushed the earth's surface up into these shapes and to these heights, the forces that had produced these glaciers and their movements, the forces that produced the storms we could see around us, compared to these things the force of human life seemed a tiny thing. That one light should go out here did not seem so surprising or wrong as it does at home, where all the forces seem to be under control and life seems so safe. In the mountains I felt clearly that human life is just one among many other things going on in the world, and that it is in constant struggle with many other things and that it sometimes must lose the struggle. These things are easy to forget at home. Oddly enough, seeing them clearly was not depressing or discouraging but instead gave me a greater zest for life.

And finally, we all had the consolation of knowing that Jake died at a high point in his life. He seemed to be truly happy only in the mountains, and it must have been deeply satisfying to him to be one of the first Americans to set foot in the Khumbu Icefall. There is no question but that he was enjoying life to the full when he died. It is a better way to go than many that are possible.

I don't want to give the wrong impression here. Jake's death definitely changed something. Everest was not just a lark anymore. We became more serious, especially about the icefall. Dick Pownall and Gil Roberts were with Jake on that day and narrowly escaped the same fate; Dick was pinned under a huge slab of ice which pressed on his chest and made it almost impossible to breathe, and would surely have died if Gil had not been able to free him, as well as Ang Pema who was submerged head down in the snow. Dick and Gil were severely shaken by the accident, and were not sure that they would be able to overcome their fear and go beyond Base Camp. I was slightly petrified myself; lying in my tent at Base Camp at night, hearing the noises of slumping, shifting ice, I must have asked myself a hundred times whether it was really worth it to me to go higher (even if it should turn out that I were able, which I had no way of knowing until I should try it). To accept death is not the same as to invite it.

Everyone felt the loss of Jake, the shock of death. But life surrounded the event and digested it, and the urge to climb the mountain returned. It might even be, as I heard someone say, that we had more reason than ever to climb it now.

The climbers were more than ready to push on, eager not to lose the advantage we had gained by being here early. On March 26, the third day after the accident, four men—the Barrel, Corbet, Al Auten, and Dave Dingman—once more moved up into the icefall, to finish laying out the route and to pave the way for exploration beyond the top of it. They did not quite reach the top, but continued the marking and most importantly left a dump of supplies—climbing equipment, food, gas containers—in a small tent about two thirds of the way up, for the benefit of tomorrow's team.

The next day was another beautiful one; almost everyone got into the icefall for some reason or other, even I. In the forefront Unsoeld, Whittaker, Jerstad, and the Sherpa Gombu left Base Camp with the intent to reach the top of it and have a look at the next phase of operations: the Western Cwm (pronounced "coom," it is Welsh for "valley"). Behind them were Emerson and Hornbein whose job that day was to mark the route even more clearly and to make it as passable as possible; this route was going to be used not only by skilled climbers but also by porters, carrying the many boxes of supplies which were going to be needed for life in the higher camps—and also by the psychologist, me, who by now had just about decided that he would make the attempt. Those of us coming behind were going to need help, in the form of steps cut in the ice, sometimes a rope fixed to help us up a steep pitch, and occasionally a log or two roped together to make a bridge over a crevasse.

The third group working together in the icefall this day, Sherpas under the supervision of Corbet, Gil, and the Barrel, was seeing to such bridges. Norman and Ang Dawa were along, taking movies of all this activity, popping up now and then in surprising places in order to get unusual shots. I came along with this group, roped together with Gil, for the sake of finding out just how much strength I had and judging whether I might be able to make the whole icefall trip on another day. We didn't go very high and I found the experience completely exhilarating. The icefall is a strange place, exotic, and wildly beautiful, and I kept asking myself if it was really I who was here, crunching over the snow, using an ice axe to pull myself over the top of small cliffs of ice, trying not to hold Gil back, and practically taking Everest in through my pores.

There was only one bad moment during the five hours we were out of camp. The route passed almost under an enormous block of ice standing on end on a small base, and looking very much as though it would topple onto its side at any moment. It was lovely, but nasty-looking, and Gil had seen a friend killed by a similar block just four days ago; he was not in much of a mood to stop and admire its beauty. He wanted to rush past it and cut down our chances of being in its path if it fell. I found I was absolutely unable to hurry at this altitude, and yet it looked bad to me too and I knew what Gil must have been feeling. So I pushed as hard as I could, to keep him from having to drag me over the snow on my stomach, and tried to make my muscles work harder even though they felt they were about to quit altogether. We got past the threat (in fact, this block was one of the few in the whole icefall that never moved while we were on the mountain!), but at the cost of two things: (1) I felt my lungs needed more air than I could possibly take in for them and they all but screamed at me for that, and on top of that I felt a kind of panic —the panic that comes from feeling you <u>have</u> to do something but you <u>can't</u>; naturally all of this passed in five minutes; (2) less painful, but more embarrassing, the effort I put into my leg muscles seemed to have taken energy away from certain other ones, and for the first time since I was about four years old I'm afraid I wet my pants slightly—not out of fear, because I was too tired to be afraid, but simply out of over-exertion! Small price to pay for the chance to see and touch such a thing as the Khumbu Icefall!

It was just as we were finishing dinner that evening in Base Camp that we got word by walkie-talkie from Whittaker, Unsoeld, and Jerstad: they were calling from <u>on top of</u> the icefall. They had broken past the first big obstacle on the mountain, and they stood on the edge of the Western Cwm. At the top they had found a tremendous wall of ice, which had to be climbed; I later heard some say they thought that the job Big Jim and Willi did in scaling this wall was the most difficult of the whole expedition.

From the low point reached right after the accident, we flew to new heights of optimism. When the lead party, as well as Hornbein and Emerson, had made their way back down through the whole icefall, arriving back in camp about 6:30 p.m., the whole group's morale was probably higher than at any other single moment during the expedition. We broke out some bottles of whiskey and celebrated. Confidence flowed back into the mess-tent; the first American eyes (except for Norman, who had been here before) had seen the Cwm; it was still March and we might even hope to make the summit sometime during April. Even I, exhausted from my first efforts in the lower icefall that day, felt like a strong man.

VALLEY OF SILENCE

The top of the icefall was reached on March 27th. The first summit team began its actual assault exactly one month later, on April 27th. Other things being equal, the move from the top of the icefall (Camp 1) to the highest camp (Camp 6) would take seven days. Why then did it take a month?

The reason had to do with the movement of supplies: logistics. The month was filled, more or less, with the pushing of a route over the snow and ice higher and higher up the mountain. The aim was to set up a series of camps at which the summit team could stop overnight on its way up, and the last one had to be high enough so that two men could hope to leave it in the early morning, make it to the top, and return to it (or to a lower camp if possible) before nightfall. Each of the camps had to be stocked with supplies—extra sleeping bags, the precious oxygen bottles, food, gas stoves—not only for the summit teams that would eventually stop there, but also for the team members and Sherpas who would go before them, setting up the higher camps.

Camp 2 was a base camp for the people pushing the route higher, to Camp 3; Camp 3 then had to be supplied so that the men working to set up 4 could use 3 as a base; and so on to the last one. Each day that the weather permitted during that month saw one or more teams of Sherpas carrying loads upwards, somewhere between Base Camp (where all the supplies started from) and higher camps. Each camp was located at a distance from the last one such that there was a good gain in altitude, but it would not be too hard for a climber to make the trip in one day. When it came time actually to strike out for the top of the mountain—of the world—each climber would need to save his strength and resources for the last stage, the trip between Camp 6 and the top and down again, and he should not have to wear himself out before getting to Camp 6.

Camp 1, the first overnight stop after Base Camp, was set up at the top of the icefall, at approximately 20,000 feet. From there the route rose gently up the Western Cwm (the Swiss in 1952 called it The Valley of Silence), detouring to avoid some very wide crevasses, over log bridges where the split in the ice could not be avoided, over a wide field of white and between Nuptse on the right side, with its awe-inspiring walls of delicately shaped and glazed ice rising some 3000 feet overhead, and Everest on the left. In front, literally looming at the head of the Cwm, was the face of Lhotse, a very steep wall on which was the origin of the whole Khumbu Glacier stretching its back beneath our feet, down to Base Camp, turning left there to push its tail several miles down the valley toward Pheriche.

Nuptse was like a jewel on which some artisan had worked for years to obtain desired patterns, while Everest was rough, untouched by design, a raw gem lying on the ground. It seemed cold, aloof, indifferent to anything going on below. But sometimes I wondered if it wasn't a little astounded, as I was, to find ants crawling up its shoulders. Indeed, it was by the principle of ants—steady, unceasing, persistent effort—that Everest was eventually climbed. The difference was that <u>all</u> ants act like ants, while only a few humans could be found who would sustain an effort to keep moving on and up under these conditions.

Camp 2 was somewhere near the middle of the Cwm, at about

21,300 feet. This was Advance Base Camp, the center of high-level operations, supply depot, control center for communications among camps, and something of a Rest & Recreation retreat for those working higher up. Advance Base was usually a busy, strategic place, with anywhere from five to ten climbers in it, and a similar number of Sherpas, at any one time—on their way up to work on higher camps from Base Camp, or on their way down to recuperate from a stay at these altitudes, or finally climbers waiting for the weather to break so they could attempt the summit.

Advance Base Camp (ABC), in the Western Cwm

Eventually I spent a month there, hardly moving outside a 50-yard radius, sharing in the moods of the climbers to whom this effort meant so much, and etching into my brain the grandeur and inhuman beauty of the spot. It came to seem, cut off as we were from civilization, almost a permanent place, like St. Louis or Berkeley, a place with a shape of its own where things go on every day of the week. Going from the mess-tent to my own tent, perhaps thirty steps, became the same experience as driving home from a restaurant (except for the difference in the food!), and eventually I felt almost as cozily at home in that little tent as I might in a comfortable apartment. It's odd to think that now, at this moment, there *is* no Camp 2, and whatever traces of it we may have left on the mountain are now moving downward with the glacier, buried under new snowfall and disappearing into crevasses that weren't there when we were.

I want to pause a moment here, while we are above 21,000 feet, and say something about altitude. What difference does altitude make?

In the process of evolution, animal and human life developed on the earth close to sea level. For that reason animals and humans are best suited for life at low altitudes. If life had begun in a different way and had first appeared on mountain tops, humans now might find it as hard to go down to the sea as they do in fact getting to mountain summits. But it didn't happen that way. If you push the process of evolution backwards in time you eventually reach the sea as the probable source of all life, and most living forms are best suited to the altitudes near sea level.

When I say "best suited" I mean that they can better find the things they need to sustain their life in the lower altitudes. In the case of animals and humans, the two things they need more than anything else are food and oxygen. Usually, in discussing what is needed for life to go on, people take the matter of getting oxygen for granted, and concentrate on the problems different animals (including us) have in obtaining food. But I am talking about climbing mountains, and as we were able to bring all our food with us and didn't have to depend on finding it or growing it, I will ignore food. It is oxygen that becomes a problem as you leave sea level and go higher on a mountaineering expedition.

The earth is wrapped in a covering of gases we call *air*, about 20 percent of which is oxygen. The closer you go to the sea the greater the weight of air pressing on you and therefore the greater the pressure of oxygen that you breathe; the closer you go to the summit of Mount Everest the less pressure, the less oxygen you take in with each breath.

The whole story of why the body needs oxygen to work properly is a very complicated one, but the main points are these: When you breathe you take in air, and the lungs take oxygen out of that air; what you breathe out is the unused part of the air and is not the same as what you breathed in. The oxygen now in the lungs is picked up by the blood, which carries it around to all parts of the body. The oxygen goes to the places where the body is growing or using energy, and one of the main users of oxygen is your muscles. It is a necessity if the food you eat is to be turned into energy and the muscles are to do their jobs for you. Without enough oxygen in our system, the food we eat simply doesn't do us any good.

The body has a number of ways of protecting itself from the threat of too little oxygen. If you go slowly from sea level to higher altitudes these defenses will go to work and gradually you will be able to tolerate the altitudes. That is one of the reasons that the long approach march from Kathmandu to Everest is a good thing; during those three weeks we went up and down so much, and raised our altitude slowly enough, that our bodies had time to make the changes necessary to operate on less oxygen. If we had flown directly from Kathmandu to Base Camp, I have no doubt that we would all have been quite sick for at least several days, and would have been slow to develop the strength and endurance that conditions demanded. In going high, it is extremely important to allow time for those changes inside the body to come about; you cannot rush them. During the Second World War, airplanes were developed that flew at great altitudes, and because one flight—from take-off to landing—was only a matter of hours, and therefore too short a time for the body to adapt itself, the crew of the plane had to have supplemental oxygen supplied to them. If a plane was flying at, say, 20,000 feet and was suddenly hit by shells so that the supplemental oxygen supply was cut off, that alone could be fatal to the crew members—even if none of them was hit directly by the shells. Compare that with the fact that we were living at Advance Base Camp at over 21,000 feet without using <u>any</u> supplemental oxygen, and you see what the benefits are of gaining altitude slowly.

This adaptation is not magic, though. You cannot do at 21,000 feet the same things you could do at sea level, or even at 12,000. I remember one evening at Camp 2, Advance Base, just before dinner, Gil and I were suffering an unusual attack of boredom, and that must have been why we decided to have a race. We ran from the lower edge of the camp to the upper edge and back, a distance of 30 or 40 yards at most, and the result was a more frantic gasping for air than I ever experienced after 440 yards at sea level. (Incidentally, Gil won, but only because I slipped and went down on one knee rounding the flag at the upper edge of camp—I insist that is the reason.) But without exertion, at least we could live there fairly comfortably.

There is just one more thing to add. It is true that the body can adapt to lesser amounts of oxygen in the air—but only up to a point. Sherpas can live comfortably at 12,000 feet; Peruvian Indians can do hard work in tin mines at 17,000. But somewhere between 18,000 and 20,000—in other words somewhere in that range of altitudes spanned by the Khumbu Icefall—you reach a point beyond which the body cannot successfully adapt itself. It can go a long way—otherwise none of us could have stayed at Advance Base as long as we did—but not all the way. Apparently, any time spent above 20,000 feet will necessarily lead to a breakdown of the body, even if slowly. Appetite will disappear, food taken in will be used less well, muscles will begin to waste away, the person will have less and less energy, and it seems that in the end, were a person to remain too long at such an altitude, they would simply be unable to get up and move around, would fall into a stupor, and if they didn't freeze to death would die eventually of starvation if nothing else. There was a time before the first summit assault—a period of 13 days—when the summit teams were sitting around Advance Base doing little except waiting for their chance to move up, and during this long period above 21,300 feet the climbers were becoming quite nervous about what was happening to their strength, even though they were doing nothing more energetic than walking to meals from their tents. They knew that deterioration was inevitable.

It is because of this limit on adaptation that our supplies included 200 tanks of oxygen for use on the last stretches of the mountain. There is no absolute line beyond which you <u>must</u> use supplemental oxygen; because it is expensive and the tanks are heavy to bring along, you simply do as much as you can without it, without at the same time tearing yourself down too much. Like a lot of other things about an expedition, it depends on how much money you have. In our case, 23,000 feet was the dividing line: below that no one used oxygen; above it everyone used it for working and for sleeping [except better-acclimated Sherpas, and climbers who ran out of it].

———

From Camp 2 on, the Expedition split itself into two smaller teams, with different goals, and what they differed on was the question of the route they wanted to take to the summit of Everest.

The British expedition of 1953, and again the Swiss in 1956, found a route to the top by way of the South Col. If you check the diagram on page X , you will see that this route goes from Camp 2 on up the Cwm to the bottom of the Lhotse face (Camp 3), then up the face about ¾ of the way (Camp 4), then diagonally across Lhotse to a little saddle between Lhotse and Everest—this is the South Col, lying at 26,000 feet, and the site of our Camp 5. From the Col this route goes up the southeast ridge of Everest, reaching first the south summit (not the true top) then dropping about 20 feet and once again rising, this time to the actual peak, the point to which all our eyes kept turning along the whole trip. Except for the Englishmen Mallory and Irving who may have reached the summit from the

Tibetan or north side in 1924, and except for the claimed success of the Chinese Communists from the north in 1960, Everest had been climbed before us only by the South Col route.

Map drawn by Dee Molenaar for Everest: The West Ridge by Thomas Hornbein, published by Mountaineers Books, Seattle

Several of the team, however, had begun talking before we left the U.S. about a completely unexplored and unattempted way up: the West Ridge, which comes out at a right angle to the line formed by the south ridge and the north ridge. While the men who chose the South Col route (mainly Big Jim, Lute, Pownall, and the Barrel) seemed most interested in getting to the top, and therefore wanted to follow the path that had been successful twice before, the men who chose the West Ridge (mainly Hornbein, Unsoeld, Emerson, and Corbet) seemed to be the ones who wanted the thrill of breaking new ground, putting feet where absolutely no one ever had before. The West Ridgers could not be as sure of their chances for success, but they were willing to sacrifice some of their chances for the sake of seeing and attempting something new and unknown. Their route, as they gradually explored it and established it, started out from Camp 2 but almost immediately turned off to the left to climb steeply almost 3000 feet onto the West Shoulder of Everest, directly above Advance Base, then along that shoulder to the long West Ridge. Both routes required enormous strength and will-power, but it seems clear that the West Ridge posed more problems and difficulties.

It was decided at Advance Base (and not without heated discussion and strong feeling) that because of logistics we could not throw equal efforts into the two routes at the same time. Since a great deal of money had been given to us for the purpose of helping to get one or more Americans to the summit, the first effort had to be put into the route that promised the best chances of success, and that meant the South Col. On the day the decision was made, April 13, the day before Easter, a team of four had just returned from the West Shoulder, where they had had their first good look at the West Ridge and had decided that it could be done.

Hornbein, Unsoeld, Dingman, and Bishop arrived in camp late in the afternoon, dragging their feet but full of optimism about their explorations. It was a great disappointment, especially to Hornbein who was the main driving force behind the West Ridge effort, to have to face within a few hours of arriving in camp the decision to attempt the South Col first. It meant that if the time required to succeed by way of the Col were too great, or if too many supplies of food and oxygen were consumed in the attempt, or if too many Sherpas were exhausted and forced to retreat to Base Camp, then their dreams and efforts so far would be wasted. In that case, as far as they were concerned they might as well not have come—and on our 53rd day out from Kathmandu that was enough to make a man feel slightly desperate.

But from another point of view the Col route was the obvious choice at this point. Even later on that same day, April 13th, Big Jim and Gombu returned from having forged their way up the Lhotse face, to the top of the Khumbu Glacier, where they set up a small tent and called it Camp 4. If the West Ridge group was optimistic, the South Col group on that night felt they were within a stone's throw of Everest's summit. And two days later, when Lute and Pownall, extending the route forward from Camp 4, succeeded in pushing on all the way to the South Col, it began to seem the mountain had almost been climbed. If the top of the icefall was the first major landmark on the mountain, the South Col was the second, and the last one until the summit itself. They were not equipped to set up Camp 5 on the Col, but the mere news that the expedition had reached its fingertip to that point fired everyone up; it proved that the problems were not too great to be handled, and once Camp 5 was set up and supplied, all that remained was Camp 6 and the summit. Time and good fortune remained on our side.

Once the South Col route was established, Big Jim, Lute, and Pownall—who had all played a major role in pioneering the route all the way from Base Camp, 8400 feet below the Col—retired to Camp 2 to recuperate and gather their strength for the coming attack on the summit. Now the job was to supply Camps 3, 4, and 5 with the things that would be needed by the first summit teams (and enough for additional ones, if possible). Sherpas carrying loads of roughly 40 pounds and <u>not</u> using oxygen did the job. The weather was only fair during these days, and there was always snowfall in the afternoon, sometimes so thick and so white that it was literally blinding.

At Advance Base we felt slightly as though we were in a sailboat becalmed; even though we knew progress was being made, it didn't seem like it, and the hour-to-hour life could hardly have been less eventful. This was the period when anything, even the Bear sleeping through breakfast, could have made news. I sat for hours, waiting for just the right shot of a Gorak poking around in our garbage heap, or

A scavenging gorak

letting my eye roam over the expanses of fluted ice stretching from the Nuptse ridge down to the Valley of Silence, or lying bathed in orange light inside a tent talking with team members.

If we had a few hours that were sunny and clear there was always much horseplay, laughing and joking in the snow, shooting silly movies, and the like; but more usually we were forced into hot tents (sometimes up to 90° F inside) by the snowfall and the lack of anything to look at outside. This was the period when Big Jim and Lute were getting concerned about deterioration, and everyone was growing very restless with too much standing around and doing nothing but waiting. On the Col route, the thrill of exploration and the spadework were over, nothing was left to justify our life here except the summit drive, and unless we could get on with that there were going to be serious problems of morale.

Lute and Big Jim

Finally, on the 26th of April, Norman and Will held a meeting after lunch, and announced they had decided that we had been sitting still, at a dangerous altitude, for too long. On the 27th, depending on the weather, either the first and second summit teams would begin their assault by moving up to Camp 3, or all the climbers at Camp 2 would retreat to Base to regain strength and morale for a week. The weather was poor all that day, depressing everyone with the indication that they would have to retreat tomorrow.

Lester at ABC, working the dials

ASSAULT - I

April 27th dawned clear and got better as the day wore on. Even the West Ridgers were delighted, because in no case could they make their big push until the summit had been reached by the Col route. And today—contrary to expectations—was the day to begin that effort. In a heat that seemed strange, surrounded as we were by more ice and snow than most people see in a lifetime, final preparations were made. Special attention was given to dressing by the summit teams, so that no loose crampon or badly fitting boot might hamper their efforts now. Last minute notes to wives were written, each pack was carefully loaded with necessities and with those special few items that a climber might want to have with him on a possibly historic moment several days off, when he might be standing on the spot to which everything had been leading. Lethargy and boredom disappeared; Camp 2 came alive again. Those of us who would not be a part of the events now beginning rushed around taking pictures, trying to be useful, trying to work off the excitement that today's good weather had generated. If the weeks and months of planning and preparing had been carried out properly, and if the weather held, the only thing that now mattered was the ability to keep pushing upwards until there was no place to go but down.

The first summit team consisted of Big Jim and Gombu, and also Norman and Ang Dawa. It was generally agreed that on the basis of his experience, past record, and work done so far on the Col route that Whittaker should have this position. Norman, on the other hand, was not an obvious choice for the first team.

A Sherpa, tightening his crampons, ABC

He was one of the oldest team members and could not demand as much from his body as a younger man could, in spite of his experience. But we had promised the National Geographic Society that we would make a movie of the climb, and Doody who was to do the camera work had been laid flat by a blood clot in his leg (which could have killed him if it had gotten loose and moved to his lungs).

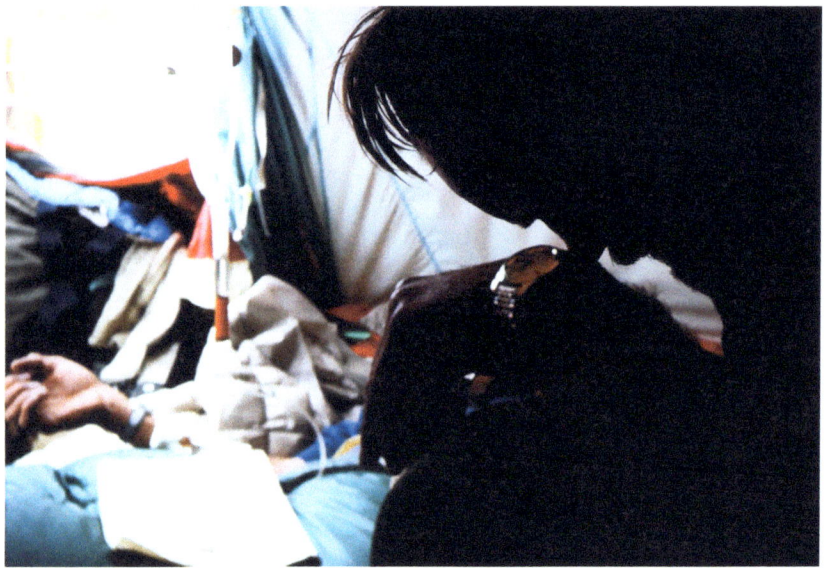

Gil Roberts treating Dan Doody's thrombophlebitis, ABC

Only Norman had the camera skills to try to shoot Big Jim and Gombu reaching the summit. As much as he wanted to go high, and wanted to produce the best movie ever made on Everest, he was not looking very eager to me as he got ready to leave Camp 2. He knew what hardships lay ahead of him.

After a great deal of flapping around the camp, amid an atmosphere like that when a great ocean liner eases away from the dock, we all shook the hands of the summit teams, and they moved out of camp and up the Cwm at that slow steady pace that altitude demands. They looked serious and thoughtful in spite of their smiles.

Jim Whittaker posing for a photo before the first summit attempt

Nawang Gombu

On the next day a second assault team made its preparations and left: Jerstad, Pownall, Bishop, and Bishop's trusted Sherpa, Girmi Dorje. If the first team returned to the Col from its efforts in good shape, successful or not successful, this second team of four would then make its own attempt. However, if the first team should run into difficulty or return exhausted, then this team would serve as a support for them, doing whatever might be necessary to help.

One day behind the second team, a third group left Camp 2. Dave Dingman and the Bear, with several supply-carrying Sherpas, moved up the Lhotse face behind the second assault team, planning to serve as support for them if needed, but if not needed, to attempt to reach the summit of Lhotse from the South Col.

While these three teams made their way up the glacier, Hornbein, Unsoeld, and Auten descended to Base Camp to recover energy for the summit attempt they hoped they would soon make via the West Ridge, and Emerson and Corbet climbed onto the West Shoulder to do some work there. Camp 2 had gone in a few days from a dead place with a high population, to a lively hopeful place with a high population, and now to a wondering place with a low population: Gil, Dan, and I, plus our Sherpa cook Danu. We watched the last figures (Dave and the Bear) leave camp, become tiny black spots against the pure white of the glacier, and crawl up the Lhotse face as the others had done, while we strained our eyes and sometimes used field glasses to follow their progress.

Danu ringing the meal gong, ABC

Dan was still recuperating flat on his back under Gil's care, and Gil was being dark and moody. Camp 2 had been evacuated in three directions, and I think we three had a feeling of having been left behind by everyone, whether they had gone up or down. The atmosphere was of a ghost time, and I could almost say that each of us was alone there.

———

The team of Big Jim and Gombu, Norman and Ang Dawa, along with eight load-carrying Sherpas who were to help set up Camp 6 and then descend, moved up to the Col uneventfully. There were some difficulties with oxygen masks and tanks, but nothing so serious as other expeditions had suffered at about this point, and nothing that couldn't be taken care of one way or another. On April 30th, for the first time in many days, the Expedition once more moved forward into territory where Americans had never been, above the South Col. Through a strong wind, blowing clouds and swirling snow around them, all twelve men moved very, very slowly upwards, over patches of snow and occasional rock, from the South Col at 26,200 feet on to the ridge that would lead them to the summit. They passed the remains of the high camps of two previous Everest expeditions, and Gombu believed they had passed the high camp from which Hillary and Tenzing had reached the summit in 1953. On the basis of this, all decided that they were high enough to pitch the last American camp. At what turned out to be about 27,450 feet above sea level, Whittaker, Gombu, and the eight other Sherpas made a little level place and set up two tents: Camp 6.

Norman and Ang Dawa laboriously took photographs from below them on the ridge—of Nuptse now lower than they were, of Lhotse behind them and only a few hundred feet higher, and of Advance Base over a mile almost directly below them. When they reached Camp 6, Dyhrenfurth was desperately exhausted, as he knew beforehand he would be. The eight Sherpas, their job done for now, left the camp and returned to the South Col, taking with them seven precious oxygen bottles, to the dismay of the summit team. These Sherpas knew that in 1956 the Sherpas who made this last carry for the Swiss had returned to the Col on oxygen, and felt they should have the same privilege, even though it seemed clear to Big Jim and Norman that they did not really need it. But even Gombu and Ang Dawa could not talk them out of it. Never mind; the team was installed on the summit ridge and tomorrow, weather and bodies permitting, they would move to the peak of the mountain.

The weather the next morning, after a night of gales and lightning, was both grim and hopeful. There was a tremendous wind and it was whipping the snow off the surface of the ridge so that Big Jim, looking out of his tent, could see no more than a few yards ahead. But looking up, rather than ahead, he could see the sky and could tell that it was a clear, sunny day. At all points below them—to Lute and the others at the Col, to Gil and me at Camp 2, and even to Hillary who at this moment was with another expedition on a nearby mountain—it appeared that the top thousand feet of Everest were submerged in a powerful storm, and we were all sure that no one would move upward from Camp 6 on this day, May 1st. What looked like heavy clouds were sweeping in circles around the peak of the pyramid, moving very fast, and the motion had shaped them into rings with fuzzy edges. There was a whistling and a moaning that sounded very close to us, though it was coming down from 7500 feet above. I had never seen weather of the kind that was going on around the summit that morning. And yet, it was a fine day. Big Jim and Gombu decided to make their big push.

They, and an hour behind them Norman and Ang Dawa, packed themselves into their clothing—undershirt, light sweater, down-filled underwear, wool shirt, down-filled jacket, a windproofed parka, and on the outside a heavy down-filled parka—and started up the ridge at about 6:15 a.m. Norman got to approximately 28,000 feet but found it a tremendous struggle, and since in such weather photography was impossible there was no good reason to continue; he knew that he would not be able physically to reach the summit, and he and Ang Dawa turned back. Big Jim and Gombu pressed on, and at about 11:30 reached the South Summit: 28,750 feet, higher now than any other mountain but still not as high as they might go.

In weather that was looking better all the time but still very windy, and in a temperature of about -30° F, the two inched along the ridge, poised on snow at the top of steep slopes that fell on either side of them for thousands of feet. The main danger now was that a chunk of the snow on which they were walking might slip off the rock ridge which lay underneath it, taking them with it; but this did not happen. At 1 p.m., each urging the other one to put the first foot upon the smooth snow there, they were on the summit, at 29,028 feet. That snow-plume of Everest that had helped us pick it out from our Royal Nepalese DC-3, over two months ago, was blowing out to the northeast from almost beneath their heavy feet. They were above the storm which was all we could see from below.

They believe they were there about twenty minutes, taking pictures of each other, planting a flag, clapping each other on the back. Jim told me later that he would not say he was exhilarated or jubilant, the way you might think someone would feel after working so hard and so long to reach exactly this goal. <u>Relief</u> is more the word for what he felt, and a sense not of personal pride or conquest but of <u>completion</u>—with his and Gombu's presence there the Expedition had accomplished the main thing it had come to do, and Jim was glad for everyone's sake that whatever happened now, the Expedition would have to be counted a success. He knew that because of this final push everyone would feel better about the effort they had put forth until now, and this seemed to be a large part of his reward on the summit.

But these thoughts were not the main ones. The wind was terrific, they could feel fingers and toes going numb, they had used up much of their physical resources getting here—and they still had to get back. Their supply of oxygen had run out on the summit, and the return—down to a little saddle, up again slightly to the South Summit, then down the long southeast ridge to the South Col—had to be made with what little oxygen they could get from the thin air. If anything went wrong at this point—a fall, a broken bone, inability to continue for any reason at all, it would be all over. No support team could do them any good.

―――――

The descent was clearly harder than the going up, and took more out of these two men—the one 6' 5", the other 5' 3"—than anything else. They strained and drove themselves, as the summits of Himalayan mountains always force climbers to do. At one point Jim fell and the rope connecting him to Gombu turned him upside down, feet facing uphill; the effort to get himself right side up and on his feet again was almost more than he could produce. To move from where he fell up to the South Summit was such an exertion that it cost him twenty breaths per step; for the first time he was not sure of his own ability to pull himself through and to get back safely.

They reached Camp 6 at about 5:45 p.m., almost twelve hours after leaving it that morning. Norman and Ang Dawa, nearly out of strength themselves, were barely able to congratulate them, and to give them hot tea, hot soup and a little solid food. The four of them could not consider any further effort that day, and contrary to the original plans they had to spend one more night at Camp 6. Even that might have been a disaster if those eight Sherpas had not come with them yesterday, carrying enough oxygen so that they now had a few bottles to use for sleeping.

There was another revision in the plans. The team that had come up the Lhotse face one day behind Jim and Norman had, by the time the first team got down to the Col, suffered the effects of two nights there already, and were running short on oxygen bottles. On the morning of May 2nd, when the four above were coming down—with great difficulty, and now without oxygen—from Camp 6 to Camp 5, the second team still did not know whether or not Jim and Gombu had made it, nor what shape they were in. They were in a position themselves to make the next attempt to go to the summit, but with their oxygen shortage they decided that only two of them —Lute and the Barrel—would try it, and these two started up the ridge to Camp 6. But when they met Whittaker and Gombu and discovered their extreme fatigue, and heard that Dyhrenfurth and Ang Dawa behind them were in even worse shape, Jerstad and Bishop knew in a moment that this was not going to be their summit day. What strength and oxygen they had left would be needed to see that the first summit team got safely down the Lhotse face again, to the relative comfort of Advance Base, and as soon as possible down to Base Camp, where it was warm, there was plenty of food, no need for extra oxygen, and the living was, relatively speaking, easy.

This was the end of the first all-out effort of the Expedition. It had both great joy in it, because of the success, and great disappointment for the second team, especially Lute and the Barrel who had gotten so close to their own triumph and yet had to turn their backs. The question of whether they would have another chance, as well as matters concerning the West Ridge, could not be decided until everyone had gotten down to Base and had time to recuperate, relax, and think the whole situation over carefully.

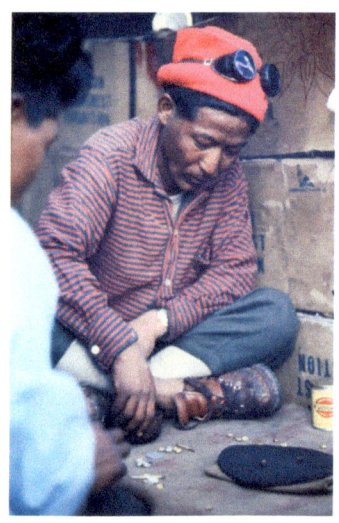

Sherpas passing the time with games at Base Camp

On May 2nd at Camp 2 we still had no news of what had happened higher up. In the morning I shot several hundred feet of movie film of Gil playing dominoes with a Sherpa, Urkien (who won five games out of six). In the afternoon, we made out the string of black figures moving slowly down the Lhotse face, and concluded that the weather had indeed been too rough and that the effort had failed. Our enthusiasm, after three weeks at Camp 2, was no longer boundless, and the thought that the whole thing was going to take much longer than we had hoped was depressing. We were in the middle of a gloomy dinner when Big Jim, Gombu, and Pownall pulled into camp with their news. Now they could begin to feel some exhilaration, and we felt it with them. We wined them and dined them with the best that Camp 2's kitchen had to offer—nothing to compare with the kind of celebrations they would get when they finally got home, but the best offer they had for the evening of May 2nd! Life was coming back. They talked about their experiences the day before, up and down the summit ridge. Gombu's English, which was ordinarily pretty good, was almost impossible to understand—he was overflowing with stories.

And the camp was overflowing with people! Almost the whole crew that had carried the assault up was now here, although Lute and the Barrel, quite exhausted, didn't arrive until perhaps 9 p.m., stumbling down by themselves from Camp 3 in the moonlight, still full of their disappointment. We had scarcely enough sleeping bags, because we had counted on people coming back in waves just as they had gone out; now they had almost all come back together (Dyhrenfurth and Dingman spent the night at Camp 4). I remember running around from tent to tent, in the bitterly cold but beautiful night, trying to see that everyone had something to sleep in and an air mattress to sleep on, savoring the feeling that at last I could do something useful again, even if only this. At one point I burst by mistake into the tent where Jim and Gombu were bedded down, and was afraid one of them might rise up and cleave me in two with an ice axe. But they were so deep in their heavy sleeping bags, and in their sleep, that I think all the ice on Nuptse might have fallen off without disturbing them.

INTERLUDE

Camp 2 exploded back into life with the return of the summit parties and their support. It soon subsided again, as the men who had spent themselves on the Col route retreated down the Cwm and icefall to Base Camp, but the life there never again fell to quite the low level reached during the last days of April.

On May 3rd, when Roberts hiked up toward Camp 3 to meet Dyhrenfurth and Dingman coming down, I was left in camp alone with the cook Danu and a single Sherpa whom Gil and I had christened "Ace," who could speak not a single word of English; or if he could he wouldn't admit it. For a few hours I felt truly alone—amidst the tremendous powers represented by Everest, Nuptse, and Lhotse, the Khumbu Glacier, and the eternal constellations that would make their appearance when the sun went down to the west of me, somewhere over India. One more time I approached that "out of this world" experience of timelessness, and it seemed to me that if, by some strange turn of things, I should be stranded alone here on the Cwm, unable to move down, I would probably meet my death without panic, giving myself up to the overwhelming spirit of the kept them from making their bid for the summit, their anger might well have ruined the ending of the expedition for everyone.

And so, from a desire to see the ones who still had it in them to go up again, and also from respect for the strong feelings of the four men who had worked and waited for their turn during the first push by Whittaker and Dyhrenfurth, the bulk of the team now prepared to "stand by" at Base, while the work began of stocking a string of camps on the West Ridge, as had been done on the Col route, and then pushing up through them.

———

For several reasons it may be that the climbing now to come would be even harder than what had been done before. Certainly everyone was in worse physical condition than in April. And the West Ridge looked, from what had been seen so far, like it posed more problems to skill and endurance than did the South Col. Our Sherpa team, too, was worn down and could not be expected to work as long or as hard as before; some of the ones who had carried to Camp 6 could simply not be pushed above Base Camp now. Personally, I felt so weak that I was astounded anyone could even consider starting up toward the peak again. It had looked so "attainable" when we first moved into Base Camp, and it looked so impossibly far above us now! But we were here, the necessary oxygen was already up on the mountain, Sherpas were available even if not as strong as before now; such an opportunity would not come again except at great expense to someone, and plainly we had to make the most of it.

———

West Ridge

This is where matters stood on the much-discussed but still untraveled West Ridge route. There had been some exploration, even before the decision was made to go all out on the South Col route. On

ASSAULT - II

There were mixed feelings among everyone who knew he could not be going up the mountain again—whether as with Big Jim and Pownall, because their job had been done, or as with Dan and the Bear because of physical condition; mixed feelings about staying still longer at the foot of Everest, for the sake of trying to climb it again. On May 20th it would be exactly three months since we had left Kathmandu, and thoughts of hot baths and fresh food and new faces were pressing in on many of the team.

But those who now wanted to carry the ball were motivated enough to make up for the rest of us. Hornbein had devoted uncountable hours to thinking about just how it should be done on the West Ridge, and there is no doubt I my mind that if a voting majority had overruled him and the expedition had left Base Camp without giving him a chance to test his idea and his tremendous drive, he would have carried a bitterness for years, as well as a big question mark about himself and his limits. And Jerstad and Bishop, who had once had to turn back through no fault of their own—if the desire of the rest of us for luxury and entertainment and warmth had rising full moon, and as the moon approached the Lhotse summit ridge it lighted the air above it over a wide area, making a huge silver screen on which it threw the black shadow of the Lhotse crags—black upon silver upon the black of night. As the moon rose, the silver light and these shadows became more intense and lowered themselves until they were spread out over the snow and ice of Everest and Nuptse. There they flickered and moved in slow and stately procession down toward the lower end of the Cwm, paced by the rise of the moon, changing the shape of everything, relieving us of our sense of the solidity and weight around us, giving us the illusion that everything, including the stiff-with-cold-climbers watching, was drifting supremely through space at its own whim. When the moon had made its own entry into the sky, ever so slowly revealing itself above Lhotse in almost a blast of light, climbing higher until it was finally just another full moon and we were just cold, tired men burrowing into our sleeping bags to lose the chill, I had the feeling that we had, by chance, seen a spectacle of the earth and moon enjoying each other which we were never meant to see. By itself, that evening made these days at Camp 2 more than worth the staying.

On May 9th Tom Hornbein persuaded Gil and me that for the sake of our own health we should go down on the 11th. I was suddenly sorry that I hadn't tried to go higher, even if only to Camp 3, or to 3W on the West Ridge, and sorry that I wouldn't be here to welcome down the next summit parties—for now it had been decided that two more efforts would be made: Hornbein and Unsoeld by way of the untried West Ride, and Jerstad and the Barrel by way of the South Col. With fantastic brashness the two teams even planned to try to meet on the summit. My disappointment, however, was not so strong as my relief at the idea of being in Base Camp, breathing easier, getting a change of scene, and, maybe above all, a change of diet.

place. But Gil, Norman, and Dingman were soon back, and I cut these drifting reflections short to concentrate on shooting movies of their arrival.

On the 4th I gave myself almost completely to the world of James Bond in <u>Goldfinger</u>—I drove fabulous cars, consumed delicious meals and drank expensive wines, fought with vicious enemies and defended myself against too-friendly women. It was snowing when we awoke that morning and continued through the whole day; there was nothing else to do.

Gil and I were staying here to wait for decisions about the West Ridge and about another chance for Jerstad and Bishop on the Col route. If groups of men were soon to be coming back into the Cwm then a doctor would have to be here to cover this base in case of emergencies (of which there had already been two: Dan's blood clot, and a dangerous attack of lung trouble which the Bear had when he and Dave were at Camp 4). So Gil should stay, and for the purpose of my research I wanted to be near where the action was, not out of touch with it back at Base. Both of us felt strongly that we did not want to have any more to do with the icefall than was necessary, so going down and coming back up again was out of the question, though many of the others out of necessity had done it.

Secretly I was taking a small amount of pride in being the current uppermost tip of the American Everest Expedition—no one at this point was above Advance Base and the bulk of the team was below us. But this was foolish, and now that there was no ambition here to give life some clear meaning we were getting bored and actually feeling the deterioration. We tried not to admit it. But Gil was extremely irritable, and I had lost interest even in Agent 007 and was doing little except standing around staring into the light snowfall and escaping into daydreams.

One thing worthwhile happened during this period: a perfect moonrise directly over Lhotse, a long slow-motion thing that kept me standing in the below-0° temperature for perhaps half an hour while it unfolded. The Lhotse face was directly between us and the this reconnaissance, between April 3rd and April 12th, by probing forward, coming down to rest or wait out some bad weather, and then struggling upward again, the West Ridge reconnaissance group ground its way up from Advance Base Camp to a site on the snow-covered West Shoulder, directly above Advance Base at about 23,800 feet; this was 3W (for 3-West). The snow in front of them, forward along a knife-edge line, climbed and dipped as it rose toward the exposed rock of the final summit pyramid of Everest, the rock face that gets the most wind and therefore holds the least snow. On April 12th, Hornbein, Unsoeld, and the Barrel, using oxygen now, pushed the exploration along the length of this snow-ridge, to 25,100 feet, reaching the point where the West Shoulder met the West Ridge, the bottom of the huge mound of rock at the pinnacle of which was the summit they sought. But now, mid-April, they had to return to Advance Base to report their opinion, which was that Everest <u>could</u> be climbed from this side. They were ready to do it immediately, that very week; but that afternoon the decision was made to attempt the South Col route first, with all the strength and without dividing our forces, and Hornbein and the others had to postpone their plans and sit on their ambitions.

But they kept working. During the last two weeks of April, while the main activity was on the Lhotse face and the South Col team rested and waited at Camp 2, Hornbein and Unsoeld and a small crew of Sherpas did what they could to ferry food and oxygen up to their own special supply dump, just below 3W. They could not be sure that they would in fact have the privilege of tackling the West Ridge, but they were like squirrels, hoarding everything they might need, in case...

Tom Hornbein unsheathing an oxygen cannister, ABC

Tom Hornbein and Willi Unsoeld, pioneers of the West Ridge.

While Hornbein and Unsoeld methodically figured what they

might need higher up, found ways to extract it from Advance Base Camp (where supposedly <u>all</u> supplies were being thrown into the Col effort), and themselves led their few Sherpas up and down the strenuous climb between Camp 2 and their supply-dump, Corbet and Auten went above them to 3W where they tried to set up a mechanical arrangement—a gasoline engine that should have been able to winch 500 pounds in one load from the dump to 3W. Unfortunately, after five days, not only were they unsuccessful in getting the tiny engine to work—much to their disappointment, because it could have replaced many of the Sherpas they had lost to the Col group—but they were no longer talking to each other! Such are the hidden dangers of life on a great mountain!

On the same day that Big Jim, Norman, Gombu, and Ang Dawa moved into Camp 6 above the Col (April 30th), Hornbein and Unsoeld moved down to Base for their final rest and planning. With manpower, supplies, and now even time, strictly limited, planning became as important as mountaineering skill or physical endurance. Until now, most of us had had a sense of plenty of time, because we had reached the mountain, breached the icefall, and probed as far as the South Col, much earlier than any other team. But in early May, after Big Jim and Gombu's success, when most of the team had gathered at Base Camp, it was decided that we should leave the mountain —begin the return march to Kathmandu—on May 22nd. That meant that both summit teams now had a deadline, and less than two weeks in which to "do or die." The pressure was definitely on, in a way it had not been during April.

It was particularly <u>on</u> for the West Ridge team, since they still did not know what kind of climbing they might run into above 25,000 feet; furthermore, they still had to establish and stock camps 4W, 5W, and 6W. Hornbein and Unsoeld, at Base Camp, hardly came out of their tent and spent almost all their waking minutes perfecting the details of their attack.

On May 6th, bursting with energy and enthusiasm, the two of them stormed up through the icefall and made it all the way to Camp

2 in one day—a long haul, yet they hardly seemed fazed by it when they arrived. They were in high gear now, and not coasting along behind someone else. The rest of their team—Corbet, Emerson, and Auten—were here too, and together with their Sherpas they immediately went to work moving their supply loads from their dump up to 3W. On May 13th there was nothing more to move up, and 3W became their base of operations, their own Advance Base.

On the 14th, loads were carried to camp 4W, which they had last seen over a month ago. <u>Then</u> they had been unsure they would get back to it; <u>now</u> here they were, the weather was good—the mountain seemed almost to be encouraging them, and they needed it. On the 16th, while loads were moved up behind them, Hornbein and Unsoeld climbed out of Camp 4W onto the rock above it—the first men ever to do so—and in the afternoon reached a point at 26,000 feet, exactly the same altitude as the South Col. They were surprised to have gotten so far, and very encouraged about the still-unknown rock that lay above them—rock that might be either an absolute barrier or a stairway to the summit. The next few days would tell.

It sometimes seems that things are most likely to go against you just when you have the highest spirits. On the night of the 16th, a large group was sleeping at 4W: Hornbein and Unsoeld, Corbet and Auten, and four Sherpas. At midnight, hell broke loose. Corbet and Auten awoke confused, then realized that their whole tent was sliding downhill, under sail in front of a tremendous gale! And then, before they could do the slightest thing about it, they were rolling over and over, as in a space capsule gone out of control. There were three things that could have happened at this point: they might have blown to the south, in which case they would have soon been in the air, rocketing toward Camp 2 in the Cwm some 4000 feet below; or, they might have blown slightly to the north, in which case they would have a long slide rather than a free fall through space, some 6000 feet down into Tibet (at the very least this would have put them in trouble with the U.S. Passport Office, which will not let Americans enter Tibet); or finally, they could slide directly down the ridge to a little flat hollow which would stop their ride, at least for a while. That is what happened. So close did we come to adding six more names to the list of those who have died on Everest.

But it was only midnight, and the storm was just building up its strength. The "mountain-nauts" did what they could to pin down their now-upside-down tent, and Auten forced his way against the winds up to Hornbein and Unsoeld, who had no way of knowing what had happened. Once they had had a look at the damage, and further battened things down, there was nothing to do but return to their own tent and hope it stayed put through the night. It did, but the West Ridge team (minus Emerson at this point) had to endure the worst storm experienced on the whole expedition. The hours until morning must have seemed like days. [Moving up more slowly, Dick was bivouacking in a crevasse farther down, below 3W, largely untroubled by the storm.]

In daylight, and once off the ridge and out of the worst of the wind, they managed to make it down to 3W. There they had to add up the extent of the damage and face the fact that they had been set back at least several days, just when time was the most critical. There was even a question whether they could find the supplies they needed to replace the tents, sleeping bags, oxygen masks, and personal clothing that had blown away that night. It would have been easy for the team to feel that their chances of making it to the top, slim to start with, were now gone, and to give up and return to Base, leaving the mountain to Jerstad and Bishop, who in a few days would be coming up it on the other side. It would have been easy—if Hornbein, smallest man on the team, had not been there with his ambition, will-power, logic, and persuasion. He provided what the others needed to make the effort seem worthwhile, and by the 20th they were ready to go again, with fresh supplies brought up to 3W by two new Sherpas from below.

The original summit date had passed, and it was not easy for Hornbein and Unsoeld by walkie-talkie to persuade Dyhrenfurth, down at Base, that they should be given those extra days and those extra Sherpas. But Hornbein's conviction carried the day; under the new plan the day set for reaching the summit—or at least for having the last try that would be made—was May 22nd. And to meet that deadline, they reduced the number of camps along the way by eliminating 5W. And Hornbein and Unsoeld would make the effort alone, with no pair climbing behind them as support. It seemed like a kind of madness, but hardly any of us could help admiring it.

———

South Col

During most of the struggles on the West Ridge route, Jerstad and Bishop were still in Base Camp. On the Col route the camps were already there, with some supplies still in them, and they could afford to make their departure from Base much later than had Hornbein and Unsoeld. After the storm and set-back on the 16th, if they were to meet on the summit, they had to revise their plans and endure a few more days of doing nothing at Advance Base. For the rest of us this was a time of sunbathing, picture-taking, reading, and generally acting as if we were on a vacation. But for Jerstad and Bishop it was a time of preparing themselves for what might be the greatest effort of their lives—and in fact, for Bishop at least, it was, and more besides. We were not finished with surprises yet.

They moved up to Camp 3 on the 18th and found the tents there buried by an ice avalanche that had come down at some time from the Lhotse face; precious energy was used digging them out. Again at Camp 4, the next night, the tents could barely be found under the snow that had drifted over them. From Camp 4 to the South Col—a trip Jerstad was making for the third time and Bishop for the second—the old steps chopped in the ice were gone and the tedious job of kicking and hacking another set of them had to be done again, so that the Sherpas behind them, carrying fantastic loads of 70 pounds at this altitude without oxygen, could move more easily.

They spent the night of May 20th on the Col, the same night that the West Ridge team spent at 4W again having carried fresh supplies to it during the day. On the 21st, exactly on the new schedule, Jerstad and Bishop worked their way up the snow from the Col to the two tiny tents of Camp 6. The weather that day was splendid; if it held through tomorrow, and there were no accidents, there could be nothing but success.

But the night was nightmarish for them; like the storm on the West Ridge, it could have stopped other men—for example, me; I am sure of that. There was a heavy wind that seemed not to whistle but to groan and almost speak. The tent flapped endlessly in the wind, reminding its occupants just how thin and flimsy it was—and yet it protected them. The worst thing was simply a feeling that came over Bishop, for no reason he knew of. He said later that he felt he was going crazy, in that tent at Camp 6. He had a tremendous desire to get out of the tent, as if there were no space in it and it was clamping shut on him; he could hardly breathe, even though his oxygen equipment was working perfectly. Even when he was lying flat, he felt as if he were badly tilted and began to feel sick. Who has not known nights when they couldn't sleep or even find a position they could stand for more than a few minutes? But this—this was something different, a kind of panic. And there was nothing they could do but wait and see if it would go away, or if it would keep them from leaving camp in the morning.

Morning came, and Bishop <u>did</u> feel better. But they had hardly begun getting ready for the day when the little gas stove Jerstad was lighting to cook some breakfast exploded with a sound like a small jet, and a burst of flame shot into the crowded little tent, singeing their beards and eyebrows, consuming Bishop's plastic (for sleeping) oxygen mask, filling the tent with bitter white smoke. Panic returned, this time to both. While Jerstad searched frantically for a knife to cut his way out of the tent and out of the suffocating smoke, Bishop ripped open the front zipper and dove out, almost unable to stop himself from pitching too far, back down toward the South Col. The stove was extinguished, and luckily they found that aside from the sleeping mask nothing had been really damaged. But the sudden exertions and emotion had completely exhausted them, and they lay in the snow, gasping to get their lungs full, for several minutes before they could re-enter the tent and begin again to get organized for their climb. This was no way to start a day, especially this one!

For the rest of the day, life for Jerstad and Bishop was an almost pitiful struggle between will—push, drive, whatever it may be—and aching, unreliable bodies. The weather could hardly have been better, and as mountains go the route was not a terribly demanding one. But if you will remember what I have said about oxygen, about the effects of going above 20,000 feet, and remember that these two men had been working hard, driving themselves upward and braking themselves back down, at altitudes well over 20,000, for almost two months now, with only a little rest at Base Camp—and remember too the kind of night Bishop had just had—if you remember all these things you will understand that the two tiny figures progressing so slowly along the southeast ridge of snow toward the summit of Everest were not two fresh, powerful young men having the time of their lives. They were two exhausted, starved, deteriorated men who were under the spell of the "magic of the summit," who felt simply they had to go on, even if it killed them. It is easy to call this crazy; but people who do so often have not looked inside themselves and seen what can be found there.

They reached the summit at about 3:30 in the afternoon (May 22nd). The flag Whittaker had planted there three weeks ago still flew with only a few tatters. Jerstad cried a little, whether from emotion at seeing this sign of life and of hope, or from relief that the end of the road from Kathmandu was reached, I don't know. The weather was perfect; they risked freezing their fingers by removing gloves (except for a light layer of nylon) in order to get a complete photographic record from the summit; Jerstad took the first movies ever made from there. They had no way of knowing what might be happening below them, on the West Ridge, but they waited 45 minutes—as long as they dared—hoping that they might see the incredible sight of two figures joining them on top from the far side of the mountain. But they saw nothing living in that direction, and without oxygen, which they were saving for the return to the Col, they could not stay longer.

———

West Ridge

On the 20th, the wind-blown camp of 4W was re-established. On the 21st, that which ordinarily would have taken three days (at least) was telescoped into one amazing day of work, and luck. Corbet and Auten, leading the way out of 4W, explored above, looking for a place as high as possible and wide enough to hold one tent, on which to set up Camp 5W, the summit springboard. Behind them came five Sherpas carrying the tents and supplies for 5W; of course, it was possible that no such campsite could be found, but if it were found there would be no time to wait another day for the supplies to reach it. And behind the Sherpas, for a while at least, came the two who would leap from the springboard if one could be found, Hornbein and Unsoeld, traveling fairly light to conserve their strength. Emerson was with them now, going as high as he could that day to wish his two best friends on the team well; but he knew that because of his trouble with the altitude—which had kept him ill for weeks—he would not be going as far as 5W, but would stop and wait for Corbet and Auten and the five Sherpas who would be returning to 4W before nightfall.

A spot—and that is the perfect word—for 5W was found at about 2 p.m., although when I look at the photograph of it that Unsoeld took that afternoon I can hardly believe that two men actually spent the night on it. The rest of the party, except for Emerson who was alone with his thoughts lower on the steep slope, arrived about 4, and immediately everyone but Hornbein and Unsoeld left, to make 4W before nightfall.

The summit pair was now at about 27,250 feet, perched precariously on the side of a mound of rock so huge that the summit could not even be seen from where they were, their route for tomorrow unknown to them—and yet they probably joked in the tent that night about one another's shortcomings, if I know them at all.

On the 22nd at 7 a.m., an hour before Jerstad and Bishop were able to get away from Camp 6, Hornbein and Unsoeld started up, leaving behind them everything but what they absolutely needed. They had no intention of returning to this spot. Compared to the Col, this route was clearly steeper and, because of the rock, trickier, not to mention somewhat longer; if they could reach the summit then it <u>certainly</u> would be madness not to descend to the Col rather than back down the West Ridge. If they could <u>not</u> reach the summit, they would <u>have</u> to attempt to retreat the same way they had come, and I think this knowledge gave them extra energy for reaching the top.

In the middle of the afternoon, Unsoeld, carrying the walkie-talkie, reached the first place he had found where they could really sit and rest, and called Whittaker at Base Camp. They were doing all right, he told Whittaker, but the trouble was that they couldn't see which way the summit might be! Should they go straight on up, or maybe turn right, or left? From 10,000 feet below, with the West Shoulder in the way, Whittaker was unable to pick out their red parkas against the rock wall above him. Most of the rest of us had climbed onto the shoulder of a mountain behind Base (Pumori) and were scanning Everest with binoculars and telephoto lenses, but we too could find neither Jerstad and Bishop, nor Hornbein and Unsoeld. We could be no help in giving directions.

They had been climbing on the West Ridge for eight hours. They had no way of telling how far the summit might be; by all rights, and by all standards of safety, they should have reached it by now. They had to decide whether or not to continue pressing toward it, against the prospects of decreasing light, oxygen, and strength. Against the dangers of going up there was the prospect of descending on this rock, which was slippery and crumbled under their hands and feet. Truly, it was six of one and half a dozen of the other, and I don't see how they could have settled it short of tossing a coin (which they didn't have)—except for one thing. At this very moment, between 3 and 3:30 p.m., Jerstad and Bishop were close to the top, pushing themselves almost beyond their own endurance because of the magic of the summit. The same thing now moved Hornbein and Unsoeld. As Hornbein put it later: "It was the old onwards and upwards; a total rejection of turning back; a total detachment from everything else in the world; only Everest was <u>there</u>. Only the summit above us, beckoning." The idea of death was a reality, but only an idea; in a sense their muscles took over from here and insisted on pushing upwards. Insofar as they could think, the only way home they could think of was over the top.

———

<u>And never the twain shall meet...</u>

With another hour and a half of climbing, at 5 p.m. Hornbein and Unsoeld reached perhaps 28,500 feet. They had been, for some time this afternoon, off the ridge and to the left of it, climbing sometimes on rock and sometimes on long patches of snow. Now they arrived back at the actual ridge-line, and suddenly for the first time were able to see where they were. They could look across at the vertical wall of Nuptse, and almost straight down at the Cwm and Advance Base, in the abyss between them and Nuptse; they could look ahead and see most of the Lhotse face. And they could see now their own West Ridge forming a clear line to the summit, joined there by the southeast ridge coming up from the Col, and the northeast ridge coming up from Tibet. It was like doing a puzzle, when you finally see how all the pieces fit together. Just another 500 feet upward and the last piece would be in place. They climbed over some very craggy rock, then were on snow again; the sun was going down and the air seemed to be pink; a stiff wind was coming up. Just 40 feet away from the summit itself they first saw what Jerstad and Bishop had seen three hours earlier that afternoon: the flag stretched tight in the wind, waiting for them.

Tom later said they were "full of unspoken thoughts and feelings—almost unfelt feelings in a way," and I'm sure it must be nearly impossible to know <u>what</u> you feel at a time like that. They had only a few minutes to take some pictures before the sun went down, to study the incomparable view and watch the shadows of the Himalayas grow to lengths of 40 or 50 miles out on the plains of Tibet. There was no question in their mind about which way they would go down; even though the descent to the Col would be as new and unfamiliar to them as the West Ridge had been for twelve hours that day, still it was a safer way to go—and somewhere ahead of them in that direction were Jerstad and Bishop; they could still see their boot prints on the summit and knew they had been there before them. They started down about 6:30, in much better condition and spirits than Jerstad and Bishop before them, but still unable to tell where they might spend the coming night. They hoped to make Camp 6 above the Col if possible.

Jerstad and Bishop had left the summit at about 4:15. Apparently they had barely enough strength to move at all, and they were limiting themselves to only a tiny flow of oxygen so as to make it last. Like Whittaker before them when he had his fall near the South Summit, they wondered now whether they really were going to make it at all. Near-total exhaustion is almost impossible to imagine; reading about it you are likely to think "Well, I know it was rough but <u>I</u> could have kept going, <u>I</u> could have found the extra stuff to get me down safely." But no; when your resources are gone they are simply gone. There comes a time when you simply sag and say, Let come what may, I can do no more. And then in the next moment you find that you <u>can</u> do a little more, only to reach the end of your rope once again—and again, and again.

Stumbling down the sharp ridge, with the threat of a fatal fall just feet on either side of them, a strong wind blowing fine snow inside their goggles and half-blinding them, with darkness settling onto them like a blanket, Jerstad and Bishop were now in an extremely dangerous situation. At 8 p.m. they were still at about 28,400 feet, still a thousand feet above Camp 6 and the welcoming support of Dingman and Girmi; they had come only 600 feet down from the summit in the last three and a half hours. They were stopped. Bishop listened to the wind, thinking, as he had thought before, that he could hear a voice calling or shouting. The wind died for a few seconds, and even in the stillness he heard the shout. Jerstad could hear it too. Just when they were at the edge of endurance, when they most needed another human being, here was one! They thought it must be Dingman or Girmi coming up the ridge to look for them, until they realized the voice was coming from <u>above</u> them—it had to be Hornbein and Unsoeld, catching up with them!

The West Ridge summit team was able to push itself harder along the descent and had made good time—they reached the South Summit, at 28,750 feet, in only 45 minutes. For a while they had enough light to see the footprints of the pair that had gone ahead of them by several hours, but they kept losing the track, first in places where rock stuck up through the snow and later because it was too dark to see anything. Now they had no way to measure their progress or even to know if they were actually staying on the ridge, and they knew the dangers of drifting to one side or the other. Camp 6 might be one hour or eight hours away, they couldn't tell; nor could they know that Jerstad and Bishop were just ahead of them, even more unsure than they of whether or not to keep going against the risks. Hornbein and Unsoeld tried shouting, in hopes of reaching Dingman and Girmi if they should be close (which they weren't). And it was these shouts that reached Bishop, then Jerstad.

From the time each pair realized there was another pair near them, it took two hours for them to get together. In the blackness the going was extremely slow; Jerstad and Bishop stayed put, shuffling their feet to keep some blood flowing in them, shouting to the others to help them find their way down to them. It was after 9:30 when they all embraced, almost desperately happy to have company on that night; it was only after the back-pounding that Hornbein and Unsoeld discovered it was Jerstad and Bishop they were with, and not Dingman and Girmi.

The joy and comfort of meeting gave them strength, and they pressed on down the ridge, Jerstad and Bishop tied together behind Hornbein and Unsoeld tied together. It wasn't long before Hornbein and Unsoeld realized how close to their own absolute limits Jerstad and Bishop were, and how little able the South Col team would be able to lead the West Ridgers down this descent. They were simply four little dots of will-power, stranded almost in space even though their feet were solidly on the ground. They kept moving slowly, and once Jerstad did in fact slip, saved only by catching on the rope between Tom and Willi. They reached the end of the knife-edge part of the ridge and groped their way along a surface that was somewhat flatter and wider; but in the jumble of snow and rock, finding the way was even harder than on the ridge, and the threat that their next step would be into air was increased. What kept them going? The summit no longer held any magic. Nothing but the most basic kind of drive for self-preservation could have provided what little energy they found in themselves.

At half an hour past midnight they were still above 28,000 feet and so unsure of their movements that everything came to a halt. They hardly needed to discuss it—for that matter they could hardly speak. But no one needed to be persuaded that to go on would be almost as dangerous as to walk the railing of the Golden Gate Bridge blindfolded; in other words, it would probably be suicide. They stopped, found a small level area of rock sticking out of the snow, and huddled together on it for the rest of the night.

———

The night of May 22nd had been the kind of night that must come only a few times a year near the top of Everest. The wind died down, there were no clouds, and though the temperature was probably around 18° below zero, still the conditions were as favorable to living creatures as they possibly could have been. If there had been severe winds, or heavy snowfall, there might still be four frozen bodies where the two summit pairs sat down to spend the night.

Jerstad and Bishop were motionless. They probably slept some, though it is hard now for them to recall. They had nothing left to give, even for their own survival. Hornbein and Unsoeld were able to wiggle fingers and toes and to help one another stay warm, though they probably dozed off from time to time, too.

Day began to dawn around 4 a.m. By 5, all were awake, staring out at the clear windless day that the sun was bringing to life, recognizing that they were still alive, even recognizing that this dawn was possibly the most inspiring they would ever see. They watched the sun rise from the most commanding spot in the world, and about 5:30 they too began to rise. There was no tent to take down, no camp to break. Still roped together, they shook themselves and moved around a bit to loosen some of the stiffness, and moved down, Tom and Willi a bit ahead of Jerstad and Bishop. They were still a long way from Base Camp, and an unthinkably long way from Kathmandu. But they were still alive, and very close to human help in the form of Dingman and Girmi, who met them about 6:30 or 7, gave them oxygen and helped them down to Camp 6.

A sudden attack of bad weather on this day would have been a disaster. But the day was glorious, and Dingman's support team including two Sherpas urged the four others down, down to the Col for a rest and some nourishment there, then down across the top of the Lhotse face to Camp 4 and beyond. At 5 in the afternoon, the struggling band was somewhere between Camps 4 and 3 at the regular hour for walkie-talkie contact between parties on the mountain. Amazingly, Unsoeld's walkie-talkie was working. Not only did he reach Advance Base to let Miller and Jimmy Roberts, who would help them thaw their feet, know they were coming for the night, but they also reached us at Base Camp. And this walkie-talkie contact came at just the same time that Doody was talking on the big radio with Kathmandu, so that Unsoeld and Bishop, still not out of trouble, were able to send messages through Doody to their wives who were both there in the radio shack in Kathmandu—and the men on the Lhotse face could receive their first congratulations from their families and from the world.

They reached Advance Base about 10:30 that night. I wish I had been there to greet them and talk with them. But maybe there wasn't much talking at that point. Dingman examined their feet and found that only Hornbein's had apparently not been severely frozen. Jerstad's were not so bad as Unsoeld's and Bishop's, and it seemed very likely even at that point that for those two the loss of most of their toes was probable.

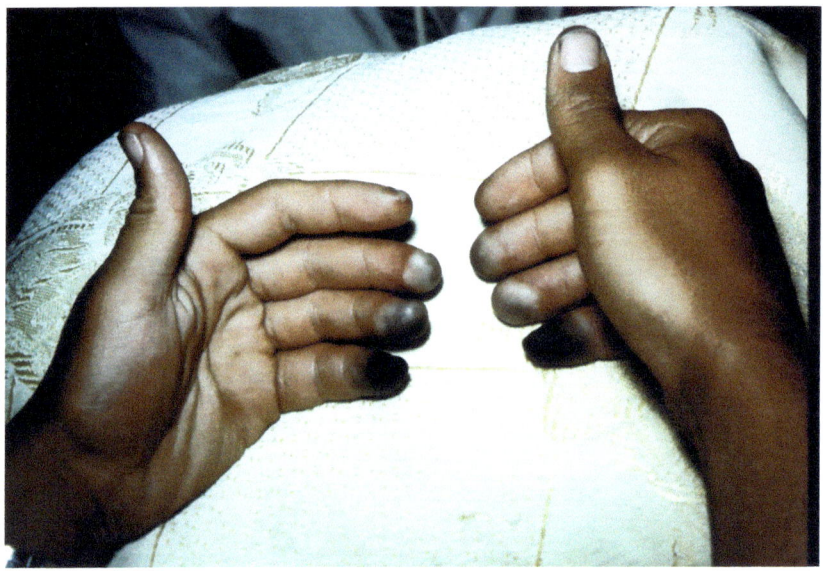

Frostbitten fingers of unidentified Sherpa

The next day, the weather continued to hold, and Advance Base Camp was finally closed up. Everyone left it, some now on thawed feet that were intensely painful with the return of feeling. They all kept moving, descending to Camp 1, then down through the icefall for the last time. I don't remember now who arrived at Base Camp first. The sun had recently dipped behind the mountains around Namche, twenty miles south of us, and we rushed out to welcome and help them into camp in a grayish light. Or maybe it was just their faces that were gray. Jerstad was able to muster a tiny smile around one corner of his mouth, while Bishop kept his eyes seriously on his feet as he painfully put one in front of the other over the rocks coming into camp. Unsoeld was having more trouble than Hornbein, but both managed to give big smiles to us when we greeted them with hugs and mugs of hot tea. Dyhrenfurth assigned Ang Dawa—faithful, devoted Ang Dawa—to run his movie camera as he went out to welcome the heroes home; but Ang Dawa had been drinking chang since early in the afternoon and was now feeling no pain; I saw him look through the view-finder and start it rolling, but then he seemed to forget it was a camera and knocked it gently spinning on its tripod as he left his post, to throw his arms around each of the four as they passed, his eyes full of joyful, drunken tears.

THE RETURN

By 9 in the evening, May 24th, almost everyone was off the mountain and for the first time since March assembled together in one camp—not only in one camp, but in one tent and practically in one another's lap. The feelings we all had—a mixture of relief at everyone's being safe and finally out of danger, concern for the feet of Unsoeld and Bishop and for the pain also of Jerstad and Hornbein, relief that the job was done, and a great desire simply to huddle together and share all these feelings—all this made it impossible for anyone *not* to want to crowd into the mess tent with the rest. The scene inside was chaos, and yet very warm and moving. No more thin little voices coming over walkie-talkies, no more worrying how the weather was going to affect the welfare of a close friend, no more straining to size up the possibilities for success—here and now in this overstuffed tent the only important thing was that people who had exposed themselves to danger, and had faced one difficulty after another *as a team,* were now off the field, as it were—the game was over and well won. I think each felt finally that he had earned the right really to relax and to relish the company of the rest of the team.

The four most recent summiteers were of course exhausted but were in good spirits and temporarily inspired by the return to all this human warmth and a sort of family feeling. Roberts and Dingman looked closely at their feet to establish just how bad the damage might be, and to judge what might be necessary in order to make the return to Kathmandu possible for them. The rest of us were full of questions, or jokes, or just anything to release a little of all the emotion that was charging the air. Jimmy Roberts was sitting in a corner on a packing case we had been using as a bookcase, getting quietly but seriously drunk. I was curious to know what he, as an Englishman, felt on this night, but I found that when he replied to my questions he made absolutely no sense whatsoever—though he seemed to think that he did, since he muttered on and on. As we talked he gradually, so slowly you could barely notice it, slipped down toward the floor, until finally like a tiny avalanche he collapsed, spilling books all around him, in the middle of which he was still sitting quietly when I decided I had to go to bed.

Miller, who had for the past two weeks been above at Camps 1 and 2 making glaciological observations, climbing into crevasses to collect samples of the ice deep down, taking measurements of the temperature of the ice at different depths, etc., managed to put the final topper on the evening. As far as he was concerned we were leaving Mount Everest too soon, and he was having to rush and work long hours in order to get done what he wanted to do; in fact, even today on the 24th he stayed behind at Camp 1 after everyone else had left for Base, taking advantage of very minute left to him. He and his Sherpas were still at the top of the icefall when darkness fell, and had to make the descent through the maze, tricky enough even in bright sunlight, with the aid of nothing but several weak flashlights! I think if this achievement had not followed the smashing success and bivouac of two nights before, he might have received more acclaim for it; as it was, hardly anyone even noticed when he came in.

———

Burning trash at Base Camp

On the next morning, the 25th, the return march was to begin. I myself felt reluctant to take leave of this spot, and I think the climbers who had fought with the mountain so much harder than I might have felt it even more strongly. We were fairly slow to rise, and there seemed to be a great deal of milling around without purpose once we were up. The porters had been arriving in Base Camp for several days and were ready to go. But Jimmy Roberts, who usually handled the organization of loading, on this morning was in the mess tent with a tremendous hangover and wouldn't come out.

Dyhrenfurth was fiddling with the radio, trying to make contact with Kathmandu, and almost everyone else seemed to be busying himself with nothing. As a result, the porters standing around waiting to take up their loads and move out were getting restless and noisy, and the discipline which had made the approach march go so smoothly began to break down. Finally, Whittaker, Doody, and I made an effort to get things in hand, and to prevent anything going wrong now which might spoil the return march for us. Each box had to be weighed, the contents more or less established (in case we should need them on the trail), a new number assigned to it if the old one could no longer be read (which was usually the case), and the number of the porter to whom it was given recorded. Three men, even with the aid of a few Sherpas, were not enough to do this job. But worse than this was the restlessness of the porters. They began to press forward, crowding us so that we could hardly work, and then fighting over who would get the lighter loads. They could see that no real authority was around, and it became a matter of everyone for himself, and herself—even little old ladies were giving as good as they got in the general melee. Whittaker, Doody, and I felt as if we were being caught in an in-coming tide, lifting us off solid ground, carrying us and our supply boxes away in uncontrollable fashion. We gave up any effort to keep track of supplies and were just glad to get a box tied up and on someone's back. This included the climbers with the worst frostbite—Unsoeld, Jerstad, and Bishop, who were carried by relays of 12 Sherpas, four per climber, for periods of 20 minutes each.

Lute Jerstad being carried back down

Somehow or other, we finally got moving, and then nothing mattered except to find our way over the boulders and to keep making progress toward civilization again. The first part of the trip from Base Camp back to Pheriche was more difficult than the last part of the day, because the winter snow had melted considerably, exposing a layer of all sizes of rock which the glacier underneath was slowly carrying down to lower altitudes. Walking over such rocks, it was impossible to find a pace and stick with it; instead, one had to pick one's way, figuring each step so as not to make a wrong one and break an ankle or a leg, and using up energy faster than one would have liked. I felt stiff and weak, but the excitement of heading home, with intimate knowledge now of a mountain that had seemed so remote and mysterious before, and with the feeling of being a member of a <u>really good team</u>, was almost enough to make my step light. And the effect of losing altitude was truly remarkable; every 500 feet—I'm tempted to say every 100 feet—that we dropped I could feel another increase in strength. All of us had lost a lot of weight; for example both Dick Emerson and I had lost about 40 pounds, which was more than the average loss. But what's more, the weight we had lost was not just fat but to a certain extent muscle as well, which is why Siri later said that strictly speaking most of us were in a state of semi-starvation by the time of the return march.

At Gorakshep we had come down off the glacier and the rocks and we were, for the first time in over two months, on solid earth, on the kind of earth from which grass, and even flowers, can grow. We stopped there for a while, stretching out in the sun, lying full out on the hard and for a change not icy ground, just wallowing in the luxuries of greenery and growing things. Bishop took off his shoes and pointed his feet toward the sun, shocking us all with the blue-black color of his toes. It was obvious now that they would need much more than sunshine to bring the color back; they would need a miracle. We lay just in front of a huge boulder on which, about six feet above the ground, was carved:

IN MEMORY OF
JOHN E. BREITENBACH
AMERICAN MT. EVEREST EXPEDITION
1963

Dyhrenfurth had arranged for this carving to be done by a local craftsman who usually carved Buddhist prayers into such rocks. By now Jake's death seemed as natural to most of us as if he had suffered a heart attack, and the memorial in stone seemed natural, too. We hardly thought of it as a measure of the obsession that had kept the team going over the last three months.

Lobuje, now completely free of snow and soon to be the highest of the summer grazing places for the Sherpa yaks, was not even a stopping place on the way out. I went by it almost without recognizing it, so different did it look in green and yellow from what it had looked like in white. Somewhere below Lobuje we got into a fog that was light at first, then became heavier. We came suddenly upon a few stone farmhouses, standing inside low stone fences, used only in the spring and summer, but with life in them now, and it was a little like a shot in the arm. The pace of life was speeding up now that we were getting closer to villages; the state of mind produced by the dragging pace at Camp 2 or even at Base Camp began to be replaced by a faster, more normal one, and although my heart was probably slowing down in reality, in my mind it seemed to be speeding up. The Sherpas must have been feeling something similar. Somewhere in the fog I overtook two of them, stumbling along the path with arms around each other, quite drunk but doing their best to look serious and coordinated as I passed them. It's a funny and somehow reassuring thing that when he's had enough to drink the Sherpa, tiger of the snows, acts just like the American truck driver who's been too long in the neighborhood bar, or the lawyer who's had too many martinis. We are indeed brothers under the skin.

We came into Pheriche around sunset. There was a glow inside us as well as outside. It seemed like an awfully long time since we had camped here last, and things had seemed so different then—not only the land itself, which now had its winter clothes off, but one another. No more questions now about how one was going to do, or how the other team members were going to do, or who would prove to be a good friend and who a boring fellow to be around. All that was settled now; almost all the questions any of us might have had about himself, or about the group, were, for the time being at least, resolved. We were free really to take in the scenery, and to appreciate the glory of going to sleep under the stars in a place like this. Because of our state of mind, Pheriche, in reality nothing but a little valley contained by some steep hills with some very large mountains not far behind, seemed now to welcome us back. Though wild and remote, it seemed to be showing us a very benign, friendly face.

    I had to get up in the very early hours of the morning that night, for several of nature's necessities; I walked some distance away from the tents and as I crouched near a stone wall, looking over the valley and at the moonlight reflected from the distant snow on the mountain walls, I felt a little like crying at having to leave the purity of such a place. I have felt something of the same thing in a pine forest in Wisconsin, or on an unpopulated lake in northern Canada, so I know it's nothing unique to Everest country. Maybe I'm just sentimental and like lonely, beautiful places. But at Pheriche my feeling was colored by the nearness of Everest, on top of everything else, and by an awareness of the intense and dramatic things that had happened so recently and so near. And maybe more than anything else, looking at the moonlit valley of Pheriche, I felt how quickly everything that had happened was now receding into the past and how little chance there was that anything like it would ever happen to me again.

    We reached Thyangboche at around noon or 1 p.m. the next day, and the decision was made to push on to Namche that afternoon. There was some grumbling about that, because everyone was tired and eager to drop his pack at the first habitation and enjoy the feeling of being back in the world again. But there was also a great and growing desire to get home as soon as possible, and the more miles we could make in a day the sooner that would be. We moved on to Namche, in a slight drizzle.

    I mentioned a miracle in connection with Bishop's toes. Our first day in Namche we had the next best thing to one. On the basis of the doctors' decision that Bishop and Unsoeld at least should be in a hospital as soon as possible, to prevent infection in the dying tissues, a special experimental radio set was taken out of its case. Hughes Aircraft Company had built it and sent it along with us for trial under field conditions, but we had done practically nothing with it on the mountain. But now, with the main radio packed away, if this experimental one could reach as far as Kathmandu we might be able—providing anyone was listening when we made the call—to arrange for a helicopter to come into Namche and pick up the two men with the most seriously frozen feet. Auten broke it out, studied it for a long time, then began trying to reach the Nepalese capital. Reception on this radio was very difficult and full of static, and although Auten thought he had heard something like a voice he was never sure. Nevertheless, over and over again he told the story in brief, of the medical decision and of our need for a helicopter. All the while a ring of Namche children sat as still as redwood trees at Auten's feet, watching and trying to understand the proceedings. Finally Auten gave up, since he could not make out whether any voice was trying to get through to him and the batteries were giving out. Unsoeld and Bishop went to bed that night not knowing whether the call for the help they needed, to prevent them from developing a serious and possibly fatal illness before they could get home, had been heard.

At about 6 the next morning I woke to a very faint buzzing sound. I lay half-awake, wondering what might be making it, until I realized that it was probably the helicopter flying up the valley toward Namche. I raced half-dressed out of the tent to find that everyone else had heard and realized the same thing! We rushed up a hill above Namche, and I remember thinking what a sad thing it was going to be if, after getting ourselves so worked up about it, the sound turned out to be something else. But no—we reached the top of the hill at just about the same time as the little "bubble"-type helicopter came up from the valley, chopping the thin air like a lost dragonfly. It circled the village several times looking for the best place to land and finally settled on the hilltop where by now all of us and most of the village had gathered. We gave the pilot a great cheer as he shut off the engine and climbed out to find out exactly what he was supposed to do here.

Child inspecting the helicopter that carried Barry Bishop and Willi Unsoeld from Namche Bazar

Bishop and Unsoeld were loaded into the tiny cockpit, and when the pilot climbed back in none of the three could move much more than an eyebrow. This aircraft was designed to carry only two, and never to such altitudes, where the air is too thin for the propeller to get a good grip on it. Before leaving Kathmandu the craft had been stripped of every piece of metal not absolutely essential, to save weight; now we would see whether or not it would be able to take off again, with its extra passengers. The pilot warmed the engine a bit, the propeller blades going around in idle circles, and then he gave it all the gas he could. The blades speeded up, the machine rocked on the ground a little, looking as though the last thing it was about to do was fly. Then it lifted off the ground, maybe as high as four feet, and that was enough. The pilot moved it into forward motion by putting the nose slightly down and the three men moved across the hilltop, just barely in the air, until they passed the edge of the cliff toward which they had headed; immediately then the pilot let the craft drop, with a suddenness that made my heart sink inside me, into the valley where the denser air would make flying easier. It looked sickeningly like a fall, but it was actually a planned and necessary maneuver. Once off the high plateau around Namche the trio had no trouble; they reached Kathmandu in about 45 minutes, a trip that would take the rest of us about ten days on foot.

———

We stayed in Namche several days, packing away our high-altitude gear and unpacking the warmer-weather clothes we had left there over two months ago. Many Tibetan refugees had heard that we were coming through; they were on the hillside all day, with thousands of trinkets and valuables spread out on blankets for us to buy. The Sherpas entertained us again, and sold us rugs their women weave—I still have three of them in my bedroom. No doubt I paid more for them than another Nepalese would have paid, but they have been worth every cent if only as a souvenir, a proof that I, just a more or less ordinary fellow from St. Louis, Missouri, was actually present in Namche. As time passes, it becomes harder and harder to recapture the actual feel and sound and look and smell of it, and it's all not much more vivid than some dream I might have had several nights ago. This is one time when I really need my souvenirs to help me remember.

The return camp at Namche

Leaving Namche, we did not exactly retrace the route of our

approach march. We had learned that several of the flimsy, temporary bridges several days ahead of us had been washed away by the spring floods resulting from the early melt-off from the Khumbu and other glaciers, and the streams were now such torrents that they were impassable without bridges. So we had to follow a slightly different route through the hills below Namche, one that did not cross so many streams, or crossed them high up before they had gained such momentum. It was a route that kept us at a higher altitude for longer than the other one, and it was somewhat discouraging, after dropping down 2,000 feet from Namche, to have to climb back up to a high point of some 14,000 feet again. There was a good deal of fog, mist, and heavy rain, which by itself would make the landscape hard to remember. On the days when we couldn't see much of anything except the path under our feet, it gave me the feeling that we weren't <u>anyplace</u>, that we were just moving our feet up and down and a treadmill was passing under us. Combined with the damp, chilly weather, and our general fatigue and run-down condition, those first days out of the high country were somewhat dreary, and one very much like the other.

Lester, a changed man, in Namche

At least I didn't have the letdown that some of the climbers had. Hornbein, for example, confessed that as he plodded along the trail on his still partly frost-bitten feet, he was feeling a definite sadness that it was all over, that the summit of Everest was now behind him. Worse than that, perhaps, he felt that in some profound way he was better suited for a life out here among the primitive and basic forces of life than back in the United States where life is so much more complicated, and compromises so much more necessary. I think, too, that in this let-down phase Hornbein was beginning to think seriously about what it all meant, why he had felt the magic of the mountain so strongly, and whether there were anything of value that he could retain from the whole experience. Personally, I felt no questions about the meaning of it all for me, and I had a truly wonderful sense of fulfillment and satisfaction with myself and the world and as far as I could tell no feeling of let-down at all. I suppose Hornbein's experience of let-down and doubt was one of the prices he has had to pay for reaching the summit of Everest.

The view of Everest from Namche Bazar

As we got lower our spirits definitely went up, but so did the temperature. When it wasn't raining it was unusually intensely hot. Our umbrellas were up all the time, to protect us against either the water or the sun, which seemed to scorch us and the land during the final week. I have never been so hot in my life, in a heat that drained what little strength we had left for moving along the trail. I can't tell you where we were on the successive days; the whole thing comes back to me only in brief vignettes that somehow stuck clearly in my memory. And two of these serve to remind me of the extremes of wetness and of dryness.

On one day there was a long descent through fog-shrouded hills, the path winding around and around until I lost all sense of what direction I might be going in; nothing was visible at any distance to help me keep an orientation. The fog became heavy mist and then a drizzle, the path became thick and slippery mud (the occasional rock in the path was even slipperier), and finally we were slogging through a complete downpour of an incredible amount of falling water. There were, as I remember, three of us together, on

Gil Roberts gets a haircut in the rain

our own, but I can't remember who they were. Somewhere along the way we decided the business of keeping going in this deluge, without falling into the mud every few steps and without getting sidetracked onto the wrong path, was just taking too much energy and wasn't worth it. And so we turned onto the first farm we came to, where we found a kind of shed outside the main house and huddled there out of the rain if not out of the cool breeze, absolutely soaked to the skin and slightly afraid of losing the rest of the group completely, which we imagined flying off to America without us. The farmer eventually realized we were there and came out to see us, but of course no communication at all was possible, so he simply sat and stared at us, from a distance of about four feet, for about 20 minutes—no doubt wondering what manner of creature we were and what we might be up to. It is doubtful that he knew anything about a foreign expedition to climb Chomolungma, and we might as well have dropped in from the moon. The rain showed no signs of easing up, and after a while under our host's gaze and with the wind chilling us, we started off again, luckily on the right track, ending up at the campsite where some life-saving soup and fresh, hot little potatoes were waiting for us.

The other vignette must have occurred some days later, lower down. I remember a very dry countryside, all brown and exposed, and walking for hours under a clear sky and a brilliant sun, sweating profusely and wondering if I could postpone for another mile or two the heat stroke I knew was coming. Just outside a tiny village I found a huge, leafy tree that looked unbelievably beautiful and inviting, and I was about to collapse under it, perhaps never to get up again, when Jimmy Roberts came along and urged me to make it into the village, where we could get some tea. I was out of water and I thought immediately of ice tea (knowing full well that there was no ice anywhere near), which was enough to get me moving again. But in town, when Jimmy led me through a little doorway and into a small dark room, with some wooden benches and a fire at one end, I felt a little as if I had signed up for Hell when the owner brought us tea that was steaming hot. About all I needed was more heat! But putting aside the theory that Jimmy, who did not mind admitting that he was not overly fond of Americans, was trying to murder me, I drank it, heavy with sugar, and I must admit that when we started off on the trail again I felt like a new man, more than grateful to Jimmy for this favor especially in view of his feelings.

Up and down, over the ridges and down to the rivers beyond we went, just as on the approach. But now the land was getting slowly but surely lower all the time. In some places, we walked through corn stalks up to our shoulders. Everything was coming to life again, as it always does in the springtime, including us. In spite of our physical condition, fatigue, various illnesses picked up on the trail, the heat and rain, and the leeches that now were out looking for blood and very frequently finding it in one or another of us, in spite of all this one could hardly help feeling better and better. As we neared Kathmandu, nostalgia took hold of me. Much as I dreamed about traveling on to Europe and then getting home again, I also felt a strong wish to stay where I was, to have this return march never return to anywhere but just wander on through the Himalayan foothills, stopping at night on a hillside from which after dark you could see the fires in distant villages, or by a broad curving river where the Sherpas would sing and the fireflies dance in great numbers. Some of Hornbein's feelings, and many of the others' about going back, had rubbed off on me. I felt this was how life was meant to be, open to the sky at night, in touch with the earth during the day, people living together amiably and with respect for each other, no cars to look out for nor telephones demanding to be picked up . . .

If life could really be like that, I think I <u>would</u> go back and stay— as in fact Jimmy has done, by retiring from the British Army in Kathmandu. But such a vision of life as I had that last week is like seeing a girl on the street and in an instant being convinced she is everything you ever thought you wanted in a girl, a fantastic combination of beauty and charm and disposition and strength who, if she only knew you, would be sure to find you the one person for her. Such an experience is only possible when you don't know the girl, when she is a passing stranger. In the same way, life on the return march could seem so glorious largely because we were only passing through, and did not have to come to grips with some of the realities of life there. I know that.

But I don't regret the vision I had. I need to feel, from time to time, what life <u>could</u> be like so that I don't take my actual life too much for granted. After all, if I had fallen into the trap of thinking that my actual life in 1961 was the only life possible for me (that's what I mean by taking it for granted) then I never would have seen Everest at all, nor Thyangboche, nor Kathmandu, nor Sherpas dancing. Without our own visions, Dyhrenfurth and I would never have gotten together. The challenge, with visions of what life might be, is to have them and keep them, and still be able to live the mostly ordinary life that one has to lead.

———

With our return to Kathmandu on June 9, 1963, which was a beginning of celebrations and parties all along the route from Nepal, through India and Europe, to Washington, D.C., it is time to end this story. The drama had had its beginning in America, its development on the approach march, its climaxes on Chomolungma, and its ending in the return to beds and meals with tablecloths at the Royal Hotel in Kathmandu. During the climb we had all been immersed in a common sea of events and shared our fate. From the return to Kathmandu we were back on the beach and each began to go his own way again, with a head and heart so full of impressions and memories that one hardly knows what to do with them. Because mine are still crowding my mind I have tried in these pages and pictures to share them with you. I hope both that they will stick in your minds for a while, and that they will now give me a little peace.

FINIS

ADDENDUM
BY ALISON

As I understand it, the only other Sherpa who had ever walked on American soil before the group that traveled with Dad was one Chumbi, who arrived with Sir Edmund Hillary in 1961, after the Silver Hut expedition. That expedition's main purpose had been to study the effects of extended high-altitude exposure on humans and then to attempt to climb Makalu (27,790 feet) without oxygen. Hillary struggled to finance the effort, but when he tagged a "Yeti search" to the proposal, the World Book board gave him a big injection of cash. If you do a search for "Chumbi" and "Yeti", you will find a range of photos and articles from the trip, not just to the United States but also to Paris, London, and Tokyo. On the britishpathe.com website there is a short video in which Chumbi imitates the cry of the Yeti, and Sir Edmund prevaricates about whether he thinks the scalp is or is not Abominable.

Dad met Chumbi in 1963, because the Sherpa accompanied AMEE all the way from Kathmandu to Namche Bazar, although he hadn't been hired either as a porter or a climber. The unusual beauty of the experience of watching him dance marked my extremely musical father deeply. He wrote:

I will never forget watching him dance one night, with a look on his face of such sweet satisfaction, contentment, and sense of union with himself and his fellow dancers, as I had never seen before.

We had reached the half-way point, about a week of hiking, between our starting point and Namche Bazar where we were looking forward to several days' rest and our first real look at Mount Everest. It had not been a very difficult day, spirits were high, our camp was on relatively flat ground so that we and our party of over 900 could spread out comfortably (which was by no means always the case). ... one could hear that something was going on over in the Sherpa camp some 150 yards away. Some of us went to bed, but those who crossed those 150 yards moved into another world, so different (I felt) from what we had just left as to be like a dream, and a better dream at that than we could have had in sleep.

Like a light breeze coming up on a summer evening, a spirit of gaiety – not boisterous but gentle and effortless – was moving through the Sherpa group. They had formed a rough circle, within which certain ones were dancing – sometimes as few as two, and sometimes as many as fifteen. The music came only from their singing, a kind of simple melodic chanting, without harmony, but with great appeal, and the rhythm was in their voices and occasionally in a neat little shuffling step done by a long chorus line. The chorus line we watched was made up mostly of our own high-altitude load carriers and climbing companions. (It is a delight to contrast this image – these hard brown men with their arms around one another's shoulders, taking small steps together in what looked rather like an underwater soft-shoe routine – with an image from several months later, that of these same men – now wrapped in heavy and bright blue down – hefting loads of 50 pounds and more, leaning and straining into the wind as they put one foot immediately in front of the other at 27,000 feet without oxygen, again moving as if under water but this time as if at the bottom of the sea.) Occasionally a woman would enter, or more accurately be encouraged into, the circle, sometimes to share it with a man, sometimes with another woman; but for the most part the evening belonged to the men, and the density of men in the circle changed from more to less and back to more again without any obvious direction, as a flock of birds will change its own composition as it goes, honoring agreements of which we know nothing.

Into this completely absorbing pattern of movement drifted Chumbi. Any difference in his dancing was entirely too subtle to be described, and yet he instantly communicated a sense of command of the situation as well as the knowledge that the command had been willingly given to him by the rest. He did not solo, and it wasn't pride –at least not as we know it – that made him so beautiful. It was simply grace and experience, and the sharing of these things. I thought of a surf-board rider who both rides on the crest of the wave and guides that wave to shore. His even and subdued movements, echoed in those of the other dancers, and above all the quiet joy in his eyes, these things spoke of a people who have somehow come upon a quality of living that is hard to find in the world and that makes a mark in one's memory.

———

In a letter written to his sister, Jane, from Base Camp on March 25th, after learning of the death of Jake Breitenbach, Dad wrote:

I moved up to Base Camp yesterday and found the most unfortunate news that one of our climbers was <u>killed</u> on the 23rd, when a huge block of ice slipped onto him. A Sherpa was hurt, too, as was one other climber, but the latter's injuries are nothing compared to the psychological effect on him of being so close to being killed. A third climber was just a few feet behind and was able to free the second and the Sherpa from the iceblock, but the first was completely buried and no doubt died instantly. Now the two that came so close are really shook up and not sure that they can do any more climbing, on this expedition or any other. For a study on stress, such as mine, all of this is perfect (excluding the death, of course). But I sure hope I'm not called upon to rehabilitate these two climbers, because between you and me I think their attitude to quit climbing is the only sensible one, under the circumstances. But they are really in a bind now, feeling both great fear and reluctance to expose themselves again, and the commitment they have to get Everest climbed.

In any case it was a freak accident and the first time anyone, in hundreds of trips up through the icefall, has ever been hurt there, much less killed. Most of the climbers are undaunted and the effort continues, more or less as if nothing had happened – it has to! I cannot decide if I think these men are mad, or a particularly noble breed ---

In a September 1, 1998, email to Dad, Lute Jerstad wrote:

Do you remember that before Jake, Gil and Dick went up into the icefall, we talked about what perceived danger we thought we saw the day before? We described the ice cliff, which we could not circumnavigate, for we were pooped after being up there about eleven hours, unacclimatized. After considerable discussion, Jake made an "off-hand" comment, something to the effect of, "Not to worry, for if anyone were to be killed, it would be Jake."

Tom Hornbein told me in a conversation in early 2022 that during AMEE's 40th anniversary reunion, Gil Roberts asked Dad if he could speak with him privately. Possibly because Dad and Tom had also been planning to spend some time together and time was short, Dad asked Gil if he minded if Tom joined them. Gil agreed, and they sat down together at the lodge. Gil proceeded to unburden himself of the self-reproach he'd felt since Jake's death, when he found it impossible to push himself much farther up the mountain than Advance Base Camp. It is clear now that the dark moods that Dad described when they were together there were the product of a very painful struggle.

PART TWO
ROLE REVERSAL
1963

A note from Alison: Perhaps put the book down for a spell. The tone is about to change, as I'm sure it must when you leave the clouds. I want you to be ready.

What you'll read next is Dad's memories of his trip across the U.S. with five Sherpas and the expedition liaison officer. I know that he wrote it all down at some point in 1964. I don't know if he did this because he hadn't kept a journal along the way and was beginning to forget the details or if he was planning to adapt it to offer as an article somewhere.

ROLE REVERSAL

My second contact with Sherpas gave me an unusual window on their often winning ways. In the summer of 1963, immediately after the expedition, six Nepalese members of the American Mount Everest Expedition (AMEE) were brought to the U.S. and treated to an eight-week tour of the country, under the auspices of the U.S. State Department. Five of these six were Sherpas, including Nawang Gombu who had reached the summit of Everest on May 1st together with Jim Whittaker. I became a Sherpa guide, in the sense that I was their route-planner, chauffeur, interpreter, bill-payer, and, I like to think, comrade.

During the expedition I have to admit that for me the Sherpas were an almost peripheral element. They weren't peripheral at all, of course; they were absolutely essential. But my research had me entirely focused on the team members, their behavior and their interactions with each other. Language, too, was a nearly complete barrier, and I recognized later that few of the team, who had their own preoccupations, made any effort to overcome that obstacle.

Back L-R: Noddy Rana, Ang Dawa, Nima Tenzing, Girmi Dorje; front L-R: Ila Tsering, Nawang Gombu, Jim Lester

So, they were always around, coming and going, sometimes carrying epic loads to very high altitudes, obviously enjoying one another and sometimes us, and for the most part having a good time, but I simply gave them little mind-room. It was a surprise to find that the job of shepherding a small group of Sherpas on a goodwill trip across the continent fell to me.

Some things were arranged for them, in a formal sort of way, such as the dinner party at the Nepalese Embassy in Washington, and the visit to the bowels of a coal mine in West Virginia, but many more simply happened. And they happened because everywhere we went people were infatuated with them. They radiated something that warmed one up, and everyone who met them was enormously charmed. It wasn't just that they were nice guys; there is more to it than that. They somehow expressed a subtle but surely different perspective on life from what one is used to meeting day to day in America. In Wyoming after spending a day with them—hiking and rock-scrambling, capped by a ranch-style cookout with steaks and beer—a young climber said to me that contact with them had somehow refreshed him, had reminded him "what enthusiasm is and how much fun life can actually be." (The phrase "the dynamics of encounter" can suggest that there may be more to what is going on than is expressed in a person's words. For example, I felt sure that this young climber, like many others I met in the 1960's, wanted to believe in the importance of enthusiasm, and wanted to believe that life should mainly be fun; being with these Sherpas didn't so much "remind" him of these things as they held out hope that it wasn't misguided to want them.) To many of the 17 Americans who got to know them on the Sherpas' own home ground, they represented a way of living that had an enormous appeal, because it seemed to be almost entirely free of the "slow stain" of civilization—or at least of Western civilization—and as escaping this "stain" is an important part of climbing for many of this breed, these very appealing little men became living encouragement for the hope of expressing certain ideals back in America, amid the contaminations of mass conformity, loss of personal identity, and above all the apparent fading of spontaneity and the withering of genuineness.

They had an impact on Americans here at home, too, and on people who were not so obviously searching for an alternative to the conventional, highly publicized American way of life—on store clerks, on people who met them casually and for only a moment at cocktail parties, on motel owners where we stayed.

But for the most part, the responses they got in America were simply the human equivalent of dogs wagging their tails at one another. One shy grin from Ang Dawa and one was hooked on him, from then on trying to get another out of him—and totally incredulous when told that just a few months earlier he had carried a load of nearly half his own weight to some 28,000 feet. Or Nima Tenzing, with the one drooping eye-lid that was his legacy from a childhood encounter with the horn of an irritable yak—Nima would light up as soon as someone approached him for a conversation, even though the chances were he wouldn't understand a tenth of it. Sometimes, in the middle of a sophisticated gathering at which the men were very much on their good behavior, nodding at the right places in conversations they didn't understand and looking as sharp as Englishmen at a wedding in their new suits and shoes, I could find a clamoring impulse in me to give one of them a big hug and let him know how glad I was he existed. I don't think I'm the only one who felt such things, superficial though they had to be, toward one or another of these "tigers of the snows."

The idea behind this Sherpa expedition to America was presumably to give something back to Nepal in return for its government's permission to enter and to travel through the country, and for its hospitality during our stay. In hindsight I strongly suspect there was something much more political behind the gesture. Nepal has a border in common with Tibet, which means with China, and a friendly relationship with Nepal could mean access to that border region, from which certain kinds of information about China could be gathered. Several years after AMEE some of the team-members and several of our Sherpas were involved in just such an intelligence operation, which I'll detail a bit more later. Most likely the Sherpas and I were unwitting pawns in some such maneuvering, but it was irrelevant to our enjoyment.

All of the team-members would have been happy if we could have brought back with us every man who served us, contributing his physical strength and his personality to our welfare. But there were 37 of them and the U.S. State Department was not willing to go that far. Originally the plan was to bring back five, to be selected by vote of the team-members on the basis of 1) performance on the climb, 2) personality (we wanted the group to make a good impression at home), and 3) age (we wanted those who made the trip to be young enough to have plenty of time left to digest the experience and to communicate it to others). But when we actually came to grips with the voting it became clear that each climber had his favorites, and a sometimes heated debate was required before even the number of eligibles was made manageable. Given the purpose of the trip, there were two almost inevitable choices. One was Nawang Gombu, the Darjeeling Sherpa, whose spirit plus his small but serviceable command of English put him in a good position to endear himself to the team-members, and whose ambition and drive had gotten him to the summit. The other was Noddy (otherwise known, more appropriately to his station in life, as Captain Prabakher Shumshere J. B. Rana), a non-Sherpa Nepalese from Kathmandu, officer in the Royal Nepalese Army, a climber himself (having been to the summit of Annapurna IV), and on our Expedition the liaison officer between us and the government. The presence of such a liaison officer is required by His Majesty King Mahendra, but his function is very general and vague; we heard many stories of other liaison officers who left their expeditions in Namche Bazar, to await their return there in relative comfort and within arm's reach of some very potent local recreational drinks. But Noddy was with us all the way, involving himself with the problems of the trip and making himself extremely useful also as liaison between the American contingent and the remaining porters and Sherpas; our gesture of gratitude to Nepal would have been inept had he not been invited on the trip to the U.S. Furthermore, he could serve a similar liaison purpose during the American trip. And finally, everyone wanted him. So we had two berths filled.

But choosing the other three was a problem. In the end the total number was happily expanded to six, to accommodate a tie in the voting that showed no sign of being resolvable. The four remaining Sherpas invited were: Ang Dawa, smallest of the 37, personal aide to the Expedition's leader, Norman Dyhrenfurth, on this as on three previous expeditions; Girmi Dorje, personal sherpa to Barry Bishop, of the National Geographic, and devoted to him; Nima Tenzing, of the yak-damaged eye-lid; and Ila Tsering, for whom this was his first expedition and who had demonstrated his courage in dealing with the accident that killed Jake Breitenbach. Nima Tenzing, incidentally, was Jake's personal sherpa; the day after Jake was buried under a huge piece of ice, Nima was found lying in Jake's sleeping bag, crying out of a sense of personal loss—such was the involvement of many of the Sherpas in the expedition.

Although these six were chosen while we were still on the return march, most of our complement of Sherpas made the march back to Kathmandu with us and helped in the final packing-up for the return to the States. And most of our six had a chance to say goodbye to family and friends before leaving for India, Europe, and the U.S. But Gombu and Ang Dawa were unable to make the trip to Darjeeling before we left, and so in the end were gone from home much longer than the rest; Gombu had even had a son born to him in Darjeeling during the expedition, whom he missed seeing until the baby was some four months old.

From Kathmandu to New Delhi (where both Americans and Sherpas were honored by a private meeting with Prime Minister Nehru), and for three weeks in Europe, the group was in the charge of Norman Dyhrenfurth. Their first stop after India was Rome, and it was here that Norman discovered that Sherpas have innate good taste in clothes; wishing not to be dictatorial and trying to avoid having the situation take on the aspect of a father outfitting his children, Norman took them into an upscale store (Norman's taste is not bad either) and turned them loose, and they went—on their very first visit to a Western store—unerringly for the most expensive things on the racks. From Rome they flew to Switzerland, where they participated in a reunion of Everest teams: the British of 1953, the Swiss of 1956, and the few members of our team who had not rushed home directly from New Delhi; and from there on to Paris and London, and finally to Washington, D.C.

In Paris there was further evidence of Sherpa good sense and taste. Much, much later in the trip Noddy told me the story of how, while they were there, he began to wonder whether absence from home was working any specific hardships on the men and suggested that perhaps some women could be found. In response, the men wanted to know how much it would cost, and then figured out how many sweaters and the like such an amount would buy, and turned the offer down in favor of the more lasting goods.

Hanging around the General Motors station wagon, L-R: Girmi Dorje, Ila Tsering, Nawang Gombu, Captain "Noddy" Rana, Ang Dawa, Nima Tenzing

Once in Washington, where the team was re-united for the formal home-coming ceremonies, there were parties and more parties, press conferences, and to crown it all a meeting on the White House lawn with President Kennedy. It was when these festivities came to an end, and Norman headed back to California to begin work editing the movie film shot on the climb (the edited film became the first of the now-familiar National Geographic "specials"), that I moved into the driver's seat of the beautiful white Chevrolet station wagon loaned by General Motors for the trip, and we came to grips with the problems of where, actually, to go.

Put yourself in my position: a liberal amount of money is available and time (about eight weeks) is the limiting factor; your visitors are seeing the United States (and some of them, the world of the West) for the first time; what are the places and things you feel they must see? The problem is much like that of choosing a handful of Sherpas out of 37 in the first place. There were good reasons to go to every conceivable section of the country, and everyone I talked to had his or her own idea of what would be interesting to a Sherpa.

In actual fact, there were certain limitations on our route, mainly in an agreed-upon plan to visit several of the team-members in their hometowns along the way: Dan Doody in Connecticut; Dick Pownall in Denver; Barry Corbet in Jackson Hole, Wyoming; Jim Whittaker, Tom Hornbein and Dick Emerson in Seattle; Will Siri in San Francisco; and finally Norman Dyhrenfurth in Los Angeles. The problem really was what to do and see in between those points. I debated all suggestions, and my own inclinations, but in the end it seemed to me that as absolutely everything was going to be completely new to them, any sample of America that exposed them to some differences in geography, in size of community, in ways of making a living, would have the same end-effect as any other. And I knew that a tour that was too full of plans and commitments and appointments would be more depressing than enlightening to a Sherpa, used as he is to taking life as it comes and calling most of his time his own.

So I relaxed and resolved that if the sights and sounds they were about to take in were going to be unfamiliar, at least the way in which we went about taking them in would be familiar—which is to say, casual, with plenty of time between "events" for the give-and-take and enjoyment of one another that characterizes their life at home.

———

We headed first of all for New York City, leaving Washington about 5:30 a.m. It was on a lovely traffic-free stretch of parkway, in the dawn's early light, that I had my first opportunity to expose my charges to something with which they were totally unfamiliar. Most of them were sleeping, as they usually did very soon after we hit the road for a new destination, when I noticed a growing red light behind us. I woke everyone and gave a short lecture, which had to be translated from time to time by Noddy or Gombu, on the Nature and Habits of Policemen, which I ended dramatically by pulling over, getting out, and having an actual conversation with one. This was quite exciting to everyone, though as there is no equivalent whatsoever for the role of Policeman in Sherpa-land, the only thing they could perceive was that something out of the ordinary was going on. Girmi got some good photographs, out of the back window, of me talking animatedly with the state trooper, and finally my carful of giggling brown faces attracted the trooper's attention. Gombu, recognizing that here was some kind of trouble, put on a straight face and joined me to see whether his presence might do any good. In fact it did, and the scene ended with Gombu shaking the trooper's hand and thanking him for not giving us a ticket while the trooper in turn thanked Gombu for the privilege of shaking the hand of a man who had climbed Mount Everest, and from everyone's point of view all ended well.

For the rest of the whole trip the atmosphere inside the car was enlivened by the Sherpas' sense of a lively game going on between me and the police. Sometimes they were on my side, sometimes on the police's, but always they managed to extract a maximum amount of fun out of the situation. They learned gradually which, out of the almost overwhelming profusion of road signs, announced the speed limit and they repeatedly read them aloud to me; Gombu's voice calling out the numbers as we approached a town reminded me of Mark Twain calling out Mississippi soundings to his captain. But they also seemed delighted when Noddy reported to them that the number on the speedometer exceeded the number on the signs. I suspect they were not on either side, but just wanted to keep the game from ending—that sounds like them.

New York had been largely a matter of press luncheons, dinners in fancy restaurants, and such essentials as a boat trip around the harbor. Americans we met were terribly interested and generous with their time; but for the most part they all shared an apparently irresistible impulse to impress the Sherpas. They wanted to see looks of wonder and awe on their faces and, I suppose, to feel the national pride that is stimulated when a foreigner praises something about one's country. There were many offers to take them to the top of the Empire State building, down into Grand Central Station, and the like. But I noticed when they returned from these excursions to our most "impressive" sights that they were far from impressed and sometimes even seemed to have lost some of their bubbly enthusiasm. No doubt I was super-sensitive at this early stage of the trip, because the men were being especially polite and non-committal in front of everyone and I was having to strain for clues as to what kinds of things I ought to maximize and minimize for them. But it seemed clear that efforts to evoke amazement in them almost always disappointed the enthusiastic person who wanted to help make their trip a success. I have the impression that nothing really "impressed" them or made them feel what we know as awe, the kind of feeling all of us had when we first saw Everest with its plume of cloud forming to the windward of it. My Sherpas were forever ready to be delighted or to have fun with something, but what we usually call "getting a sense of one's own insignificance" seemed as foreign to them as America itself, and experiences which we usually associate with making one feel insignificant seemed only to depress them slightly.

There was one thing that always got them. They were wild about window-shopping, just strolling down the avenue—any avenue—and observing the really fantastic variety of objects offered in the windows. I could make our stay in any town a success by giving them

Girmi Dorje browsing children's shoes

an afternoon on their own for this kind of strolling.

They were really not interested in buying or acquiring but they certainly appreciated and delighted in the scope of goods available. Remembering that above all else, perhaps, the Sherpas have been traders and middlemen between the Tibetans (from whom they are descended) and the agricultural lowland Nepalese; remembering the thinly disguised twinkle with which they watched Tibetan refugees gouge us on the hill above Namche for odds and ends worth nothing locally; recalling our Sherpa, Pasang Phutar, pulling out rug after rug from his astonishing inventory and haggling unconcernedly over price with us in the center of a group of Buddhist monks all praying aloud for brethren recently lost in an avalanche, I realized that window-shopping should have been an obvious ingredient for their tour.

Window shopping on Fifth Avenue, New York – possibly Nima Tenzing

Nima Tenzing and Nawang Gombu fooling around with coats

Gombu's day was made one afternoon in New York when he found a knee-length winter jacket he liked, and discovered on the label the trade name "Sherpa-coat"! It might have ended there, with laughter all around, but Gombu chose to ask the salesclerk if he could tell him what Sherpa meant—and found the clerk had no idea! For this merry crew, swamped with recognition and too much attention (with the possible exception of Gombu), this was such a welcome relief, and such a comical contrast with most of their experiences so far over here, that they were still giggling about it days later.

We went to Coney Island one Friday afternoon; an amusement park seemed different enough to be worth seeing and yet closely enough related to their own way of life to make some sense to them. They all looked a bit apprehensive during the rattling and clanging of the subway

Ila Tsering at Coney Island

ride, but once there they took to it like fish to water. Their tastes were different (Ang Dawa wouldn't be caught dead on the parachute drop while Ila and Girmi had to be dragged away from it) but what they did they did with gusto. We slid, in tears with laughter, again and again down a long bumpy wooden slide and crashed harder and harder into the well at the bottom; we rode rocket ships and no one got airsick; we lost one another within a maze of mirrored walls; and we tackled the Dodgem cars. Only Nima and Gombu felt like having a go at this, though the rest were convulsed by watching them. Guiding a moving vehicle by means of a wheel was of course something without precedent in their experience, and they might as well have been behind the controls of a Boeing 747. My mental picture of Nima will never fade: stopped at right angles to the flow of traffic (no longer flowing), turning the wheel too far to the right then too far to the left and getting nowhere until the attendant straightens him out, not getting ten feet before he's stuck again, throwing his head back with a huge embarrassed grin on his face as everyone piles into one another behind him…

We accepted an invitation from Dan Doody, one of the climbers, to spend a weekend on a farm in Connecticut, and the men were grateful to get out of the city, into rolling countryside and the shade of trees. They politely viewed the farm machinery but of course no pidgin-English lecture on its functions would make it really come alive for them or make its use around Namche seem realistic; we all relaxed when we were able to give that up and get on with a huge, farm-style outdoor lunch, with beer which they liked from the very beginning, and followed by miniature golf.

The group at a farm with Dan Doody, Nawang Gombu asking the questions

Nima Tenzing, considering the cows' lot

We did visit, the next day, a dairy farm, and fell into the temptation to "impress" them with the amount of milk American cows give and with the technology of getting it from them. Again, this was always a mistake; in this instance, instead of looking at the scene from the outside and in terms of impersonal products as Westerners tend to do, they had a strong tendency to see the scene from the cow's point of view and to wince at the sight of the beasts in their rigs, plugged so unnaturally into all those hoses.

Machinery on the whole left them cold (with the exception of a Wurlitzer-style cigarette machine in New Jersey), while humans or animals almost always engaged their interest in a big way. In Washington I had taken them to the Smithsonian Institute and discovered that the replicas of airplanes, steam engines, battleships, and such got practically no hold on their imaginations, while exhibits about pre-historic creatures really caused a stir. For a while I thought my excited efforts there to convey the notion of the evolution of lifeforms actually got something new across to them, but it now seems to me in all probability they have always taken some such notion for granted. I took them on a pointed visit to the New York Planetarium and made them take a close look at a working model of our solar system; I admit I wanted to find out whether they had any conception of this sort of thing. My impression at the time was that this model was so far from how they viewed the cosmos that it made no sense to them (they fell asleep in the Planetarium's sky show).

Nawang Gombu learning to swim, West Virginia

Our first stop heading into the interior of the land was Fairmont, West Virginia. We spent a Sunday afternoon there, mostly watching Gombu thrash around in the pool in a vigorous attempt to learn to swim, a project he had begun in Washington with characteristic drive. He attracted a lovely instructress and numerous well-wishers, and demonstrated again (as if it needed demonstrating) that the squeaky wheel gets the grease. (Several of the Sherpas told me he was a Big Man but they were just Little Men; this was not necessarily a compliment).

Ang Dawa at the pool. In the background, stewardess Valerie Browne, whom Lester met on Pan Am 1.

But what we had come for was a visit to a coal mine and we got that on Monday. Outfitted in special uniforms, with headlamps, and thinking that the others certainly looked funny, we descended 1200 feet underground and traveled in a small electric train out to the end of a vein where some actual digging with heavy equipment was going on.

Lester, Ang Dawa, Mountaineer miner, Nawang Gombu, Ila Tsering, Girmi Dorje suited up to go down. Photo perhaps by Noddy Rana.

This machinery, seen in the process of doing something and producing a tangible result, was considerably more interesting to the Sherpas than the other pieces we had seen standing around abstractly in Connecticut and at the Smithsonian. Although Girmi and Ang Dawa were a little concerned about getting their fine Roman shoes clean again, I think this descent was taken in by all, in an "educational" way, better than almost anything else on the trip.

An explanation, but no eye contact, is being made

The only thing like it was an inspection of the Budweiser "beer factory" in St. Louis, and that was something of a flop since it had been mainly Gombu who pressed for it and he was desperately disappointed with it. As it turned out, his interest had been commercial; he had developed the idea that he could turn his exposure to American technology to good use back in Darjeeling, by learning how we make such good beer here and setting up a brewery at home. But the elaborate talk about temperature control, precise mixing and proportioning of ingredients—all the talk about technology—only frustrated and discouraged him. An experience, or an object, or a person, either meant something to these men in its own terms, for itself alone, or else they turned their backs on it; the school-based skills of abstracting, treating an object as an example of a general class, divorcing it from their own immediate feelings and wishes, was not prominent in them; in fact none of them had had any schooling at all. I think that was one major ingredient of their charm and impact on others, and one reason being around them seemed to make one feel he was in the presence of what psychologists might call authenticity, that he had rediscovered freshness and wholeness. In any event, it was clear that Gombu was westernized just enough to show a nascent entrepreneurial impulse, but quite insufficiently to allow him to put up with all that goes into the mechanized production of beer.

The group with a climber from Paul Petzoldt's climbing school in the Tetons, Wyoming. Photo perhaps by Noddy Rana.

Lester smiling and Ang Dawa not smiling for the camera on Grand Teton

After St. Louis we traveled across the plains of the Midwest with Denver as our goal. Denver was home to team members Dick Pownall and Al Auten, and also was the gateway to the Rockies and then on to the Tetons, where Barry Corbet was living and where several of the team had worked as climbing instructors and mountain guides. Paul Petzoldt's climbing school was full of instructors who wanted to meet and climb with the Sherpas, so we had no choice. The instructors like everyone else were taken with these mountain men, but as far as I could tell, the climbing the Sherpas had to do there was just something they endured. In truth their strong point was endurance, not technical climbing, and I think they felt at a disadvantage as the young Americans clambered up steep rock faces with mountain-goat agility.

There was a hot mid-summer's day of river-rafting, but my main memory of that is of Gombu taking over the raft from the guides, and the rest of the men trying to find relief from the burning sun.

Nawang Gombu predictably taking control on the Snake River, Wyoming

Nawang Gombu at the wheel of a Ferrari

Gombu had been dubbed "frolicking Gombu" early in the trip by Noddy, to honor (with maybe just an edge of mockery) his enthusiasm and energy and the eagerness with which he approached new experiences. He used his short body with a kind of tense abandon, throwing it into whatever he might be trying in a total way, rather as if he were attempting on a dare to flatten Sonny Liston. Whether he was bowling, swimming, trampolining, rowing a raft on the Snake River, or trying to guide a Ferrari racing car (engine off), his movements were always the same, short on refinement and long on the main-strength-and-awkwardness approach. It was his personality, but I think he was also conscious that as only the second Sherpa to summit Everest—the first was Tenzing Norgay, his uncle, who was with Hillary—he was rather famous. He was not particularly well coordinated, as it turned out, and his escapades gave his companions many a hearty laugh. They learned to simply give him the leading-man role. But they had no desire to compete with him and there seemed to be no resentment, just wry amusement.

Ang Dawa represented quite another approach. Older by possibly ten years, smaller and wirier, given to chuckles and suppressed grins rather than the belly-laugh, Ang Dawa seemed to see things in more detail and sought mastery in fine control and balance. On the trampoline in Denver (needless to say his first contact) he achieved more style and skill in ten minutes than Gombu did in thirty; at my parent's home in St. Louis he showed an interest in the piano that none of the others shared, went to it immediately each time we were there and began producing two-finger experiments that seemed to me to have in them a great responsiveness to sound. And apparently he could explore the keyboard without any trace of his usual shyness, with no thought for what others thought about what he was doing, which further made me suspect the presence of a specific talent that enabled him to lose himself in his "music." He and Gombu were in many ways a study in contrasts, much like the extrovert and introvert in our culture. It saddened me to think that even if Ang Dawa had a potential talent for music, his life had so far lacked any opportunity for developing it. I wondered how many Mozarts or Bartoks, or for that matter Marlowes or Sartres, are born and die in such places as Nepal, never knowing that they are in any way different from their fellows.

Ang Dawa at the piano in Lester's family home in St. Louis, Missouri

Girmi's special talent seemed to be relating to children. Of course they're easier than adults to be with in a foreign country, less dependent on language to make themselves understood and more likely to use body language. Everywhere we were near children I could be sure one or more would eventually take Girmi's hand or even climb up on his back, and Girmi loved it. Of the whole group Ila Tsering seemed the most retiring and I have trouble bringing up an image of him at any point on the trip. I learned later that for expedition work he came to prefer going out with Japanese to Americans, and it makes me think that on our trip he was the least comfortable with the American back-slapping, instantaneous friendship style.

Nawang Gombu ceding celebrity to Jim Whittaker in Seattle

For the next-to-last stop we headed to Seattle, where Jim Whittaker, Tom Hornbein, and Dick Emerson lived. Because Big Jim was already famous locally, and because Gombu had been on the summit with him, the news spotlight while we were there was almost entirely on the two of them. That was certainly OK with the others, who seemed to enjoy most the simpler pleasures, playing with water pistols, throwing baseballs to win big furry stuffed animals, and shopping. This makes them sound like children, which they are not. But in this unfamiliar culture they had to take their pleasures wherever they could find them.

We ended the trip in San Francisco where I turned the group back to Norman, who saw them off for their return to Nepal. For me the trip was a joyful and unexpected bonus, a wonderful dessert after the main meal of Everest, and it has given me lots of pleasure to relive them both. I still wonder what my charges made of it all.

Nawang Gombu and Jim Whittaker reunited at Whittaker's Seattle home

ADDENDUM
BY ALISON

My parents met on the Pan Am flight that took my father from Asia to Europe because my mother, then Valerie Browne, was a stewardess, working in first class on that journey. She told the purser she would lend a hand in the main cabin because the flight was full. "Take a look at this. EXCOR," said the purser, handing her the passenger list. EXCOR meant "extend extra courtesy". The names marked this way were those of the five Sherpas, Captain Noddy Rana, James Ramsey Ullman, and James Lester. Recognizing the name Tenzing immediately because, after the British success on Everest in 1953, Tenzing Norgay had been the favorite hero of her generation, she dashed off to the main cabin. She wrote in *Fasten Your Seat Belts: History and Heroism in the Pan Am Cabin* that after helping with the breakfast service, "I made my move, uttering gushy, courteous remarks like, 'I hope you enjoyed your breakfast' to the mystified Sherpas." She may have mystified the Sherpas, but she bewitched my father, who was at that point merely "one of the men with beards" to her.

She was based in New York but had let slip that she would soon be spending time in London, where her parents lived. When she got there several days later, she found a letter from "Jim Lester" for her in the Pan Am mailbox at the Kensington Palace Hotel. He was staying with his sister, and very much hoped she would call before he left on July 5th.

Call she did. And then it was his turn to magic her, so much so that when he was driving across the U.S. and she had days off, she would fly to meet him and the group wherever it was convenient. That is why, in amongst the trip photos, there are some of my mother at the pool, at the ranch, and at meals. My parents married in London in January 1964 and honeymooned in Peru (free tickets from Pan Am). My mother left New York to join my father in San Francisco. They were married 46 years, until my father's death parted them.

Valerie Browne, in six months to be Valerie Lester

Dad strangely doesn't mention the ranch the group travelled to in his notes but he took a lot of photos there. My mother wasn't the only one who wore a cowboy hat; all the Sherpas had one.

Nima Tenzing's eyelid was operated on during this trip, in Ann Arbor. The *Ann Arbor News* of July 18, 1963, included a short report of this event which said, "He underwent eye surgery yesterday at St. Joseph Hospital for an injury sustained when gored by a yak as a boy." The surgeon was Dave Dingman, one of three doctors on AMEE, who went on to become Assistant Chief of the Department of Plastic Surgery at the University of Utah. He was instrumental in founding The Wasatch Clinic for Outpatient Surgery and served as the Medical Director. A photo of Nima and Dingman having tea at Dingman's parents' house can be seen in the online archive of the Ann Arbor District Library: aadl.org/N012_1239_001

PART THREE
THE CLASS OF '63
1998

Another note from Alison: The tone is about to change again.

Coming next is Dad's rendition of the month he spent in Nepal and India searching for and interviewing Sherpa members of AMEE, 35 years after the expedition. He is now 70 years old and hoping to be able to develop his results into a book, or at the very least an in-depth article. It is his offering to the historical record, prioritizing the voices of the Sherpas, and he hasn't allowed as much of his personality into the tale as he did in the expedition chronicle. I have taken the liberty of inserting small excerpts from his journal notes and musings, to fold in a little more of his emotional response to the experience and a few more details of his surroundings than he was willing to include himself.

NAMCHE BAZAR

Most of the Sherpas who worked with the American team of 1963 were at least 20 years old at the time, so they were born no later than 1943. Many went back as far as 1930, a few even earlier. Their life stories span all the development in the Solu Khumbu, which makes them a particularly interesting group to talk to. That was why in February of 1998 I bought a seat on the Lumbini Airways flight from Kathmandu to Lukla.

> 2/15: Out to New Orleans Cafe, open air, 2nd floor deck. Recorded music, then live trio -- Nepali but doing very good imitation of Southwest funk and blues, excellent dialect! But contrast with Nepal group Emerson and I heard in '63! Then a walk - the Bourbon St. of Ktm. But so funky! Very ethnic shops, holes in wall with little Nepalis burrowed in, but also the Red Rock Cafe, DeLima Hotel, etc. Pooja Guest House, many more quaint titles. No beggars, but little boys and girls selling in a quiet voice, Tiger Balm, knives. Had the thought, re music, that the variety of the world is getting cooked in an American pop culture sauce.

Getting there was the easy part. Figuring out a strategy for tracking down the survivors among our Sherpa team was another matter. I had not learned all of their names in 1963 and wouldn't remember them if I had. I had contacted Jimmy Roberts, now quite an old man, about spending some time with him, and he agreed to set up a list of the team and to share what he knew about them—which was a lot. He led me to believe there were some 16 Sherpas still around who had been with us. It was a great disappointment to me that Jimmy died just before I took off from New York for Nepal. Jimmy knew where all the skeletons were, and had a totally unromantic view of the men and women he knew so well.

All I really had to work with was the group photograph of our Sherpas taken at the end of the expedition. I made many copies of it, and pinned my hopes on handing it around to whatever Sherpas I might find, asking them to help me find whomever they could. I knew before I left that several of them were now successful trekking entrepreneurs now living in Kathmandu, and that gave me a springboard for launching into my quest.

Sherpas of the "class of '63" poring over the group photo, Namche Bazar

With some starts and stops I managed to arrange for a guide and a porter to get me to Namche Bazar, and the guide served as my interpreter as well as well as my host at his guest house. After a week or so in Kathmandu, spent trying to track down relatives of my quarry and nervously running up and down flights of stairs to condition myself for the hiking that was to come, I took my seat on Lumbini Airways.

Lukla is a village perched like most in the region on a steep hillside, at a little over 9000 feet. It boasts a dirt air-strip, the first to have been built in remote parts of Nepal. There is no control tower, no radar, no radio contact with pilots, just a telephone connection with Kathmandu. This strip owes its existence to Sir Edmund Hillary who organized the carving of it out of the hillside in 1964, so that supplies for his building projects could be brought closer to the site before being loaded on porters' backs or on yaks. Today it's the main point of entry to the Khumbu region, and several small airlines fly regular and chartered flights into it, weather permitting. The flights handle not only trekkers and expeditions but also supplies for local businesses and the personal travel of Khumbu Sherpas and others to and from Kathmandu.

A flight into Lukla is a little out of the ordinary. The plane rises out of the Kathmandu valley and follows a route to the east similar to the one our 1963 team hiked, over a succession of ridges and valleys, the hillsides laboriously sculptured into terraces and dotted with farmhouses. The land gradually rises until the plane turns north and flies up one of these valleys, the defining ridges surprisingly close to the wingtips and now often higher than the plane. Without ever descending you are suddenly down on the Lukla strip. The upward slope of the strip slows the plane down quickly, the pilot guns the engine to push it to a level section at the top, and after a mere 35 minutes in the air you step out of the plane into a crowd of porters and prospective porters, and into a mountain environment totally different from the urban ambience of Kathmandu.

I was met here by my guide, who was a Sherpa from Namche Bazar, Sherap Zangbu, and a teenage boy who would carry my duffle bag on the trail. Sherap was to also to be my interpreter and help me find as many of the still-living Sherpas from 1963 as possible. He is in his early 40s and has worked as a trekking guide and sirdar (in charge of trekking parties) for many years. He has also done what many others in his circumstances have done, saved and borrowed and built a trekking lodge, in which I would be staying while in Namche. Before setting out on this crystal-clear morning, Sherap led me to a lodge in Lukla where we both had tea and some Tibetan bread, and I had an hour or so to digest the fact that I was, precipitously it seemed, back after a 35-year absence on the trail to Everest.

Sherap Zangbu, right, getting information

Before reading my notes for this narrative I had forgotten how nervously I anticipated this hike. From my diary of the days in Kathmandu I found any number of entries like these:

Awoke in night with much anxiety. Felt I was in over my head, stretched beyond my ability to stretch, can't deliver the goods. Should have known, DID know, had premonitions at home. Whole effort silly.

And from the trail diary:

Rests (on the trail) more and more frequent, mental focus on left-right rhythm and trying to control negative thoughts, such as, I hate this, I said I'd never do it again, I'm not sure I can make it, and, the little return I'm likely to get isn't worth it.

Well, never mind. The game was afoot and the only way out was forward.

Not far beyond Lukla the trail joins the one on which our caravan in 1963 had made its way to this point (taking some 12 days to get here). I couldn't say I remembered it in detail, but the general setting brought back a lot and I could almost remember what it felt like to be 35 and part of something big. The contrast between that foggily recaptured state of mind and the reality of this 70-year-old fellow, trudging more than trekking through the mountains, more or less alone, with only a vague sense of what he was trying to do, was oppressive and a heavier burden than the modest backpack I carried. A picture of myself as Don Quixote floated in the back of my mind as I tried to make sure I didn't sprain an ankle on the rocky trail.

The hillside on which the path runs is part of the gorge that contains the Dudh Kosi river, waters starting out from glaciers high in the Himalayas and traveling eventually down into the Ganges River and draining into the Bay of Bengal. The river gorges at these altitudes, nine- to twelve-thousand feet, are said to be among the deepest in the Himalayas. The trail from Lukla to Namche passes the confluence of two of the three major rivers in this area, the Dudh Kosi ("milk river", so called because it tends to be white with glacial silt) and the Bhote Kosi ("Tibetan river"). At this juncture Sherap pointed out to me the trail following the gorge of the Bhote Kosi which leads up to the Nangpa La, the trading route from Khumbu to Tibet. Sherap himself had not been over that pass, but his father had, with unfortunate consequences. But that is a story for later.

In James Ramsey Ullman's account of the 1963 trek, he described the several days which I was now reliving.

> The expedition had come now to the country of Solu Khumbu, and, with it, to the Dudh Kosi. ... Up to here the route had led almost due east, but at the river it veered off to the north, and northward it would continue until it reached the mountain. This was the wildest country yet encountered. For the Dudh Kosi's path was through deep clefts and winding gorges, and the trail rose and fell, rose and fell, as it climbed back and forth from the riverbed to the top of the cliffs above. Often, too, it crossed the river, on bridges even shakier than the one near Changma which had collapsed. ... Above the canyons the forests were larger and denser than before. And although the altitude was higher, they were more tropical in aspect than those previously encountered, for this was a region of greater rainfall. Indeed, the expedition, for the first time, now met with heavy rain. The Kathmandu umbrellas blossomed; the trail became a slippery mire; and at night torrents beat upon the campsite tents, all but drowning out the roar of the Dudh Kosi (pp. 76-7).

One of our team-members, Dan Doody, told this to his diary:

Eight hours of a long wet day. I noticed a string of porters passing another one who had stopped on the trail, and on coming to him I found it was one of the eleven-year-old boys who are carrying for us. He was not much taller than my waist and was obviously frightened by the muddy slope ahead. I extended my hand, which he firmly grasped with an expression of utter confidence, and he with his 60-pound load and I with my 30 pounds proceeded down the hill. All the while he was confident of the safety I was providing, and I was confident that, should he slip, we'd both go sliding off into nothing (p. 77).

As one day he did; not long after the expedition, in a similar situation, Dan and a fellow-climber with whom he was roped fell to their deaths on Mount Washington in Vermont.

My little band of three hiked for about six hours this first day, long enough, I felt, since I had taken no time for acclimatization. One of the drawbacks of starting from Lukla is that your body has both to work and also to adapt to the altitude at the same time; I was more than ready to stop when Sherap delivered us into a small lodge in a tiny village. After a short rest in the 45 square feet that constituted my room, lying in a sleeping bag on a wooden shelf, I joined a collection of people from the trail who had gathered in the kitchen of the house. Most of these were locals who all knew one another, and for several hours I could only sit quietly, try to stay warm, and bask in the conviviality of these travelers. Sherap introduced me to a man whose English though limited allowed him to tell me that he remembered our expedition coming through; he had been a child and we were the first Westerners he had seen. Hiding in the bushes and watching us with his friends, they found us frightening with our height, our beards, and, what particularly stood out to him, our huge shoes.

There was one other Westerner in the group, a woman who appeared to be speaking French with her Nepalese companion, which surprised me. It turned out that she was married to the man she was with. They had met on a trek, and he had left Solu Khumbu to live with her in Paris. They had with them their one-year-old child, bringing him home for the family to see. Sherap knew the man but hadn't seen him for several years and was surprised to learn of his marriage and removal to France. This news item, too, was a tiny encapsulation of changes in the local lifestyle.

> 2/19: Waited over an hour for dinner: rice, lentils, some soft green veggie. All this time the atmosphere was of geniality, respect, equality. I went off to bed about 7:30, into a single "room" (most of the rest slept in a dorm-type room) and crashed into the sleeping bag. The rest of the crowd came soon after. Sherap stayed downstairs on a bench, because he snores! Discovered the flashlight wouldn't work, even with changed batteries, Sherap loaned me his so I could get to crapper.

On the next day four more hours of hiking brought us to Namche Bazar. None of the fairly primitive bridges we had crossed 35 years before was still there; all had been washed away in one flood or another, and replaced with higher and more permanent ones. After crossing the last of several suspension bridges (Sherap told me a Sherpa joke: a trekker once asked a guide for the Sherpa word for "flat," and the guide answered, "bridge," this being one of the few flat surfaces to be found in Khumbu), the trail takes on a nasty slope and tortures the hiker for a couple of endless hours. As I rounded a bend in the steep and rocky trail I suddenly found myself once again gazing on the Everest-Lhotse-Nuptse massif in the distance, through a notch in the nearer ridges. My slides from 1963 had become more real in my mind than the mountain, and now here was the real thing standing out in the clear air before my very eyes, the source of untold numbers of dreams and those dreams the ultimate source of the big changes

Better bridges this time round

happening in Sherpa lives. At this moment, however, I was not in a dreaming mode.

Lester taking a break from the trek

The sudden view, together with the depressing difficulty of this stretch, brought back to me in a rush the long-forgotten, maybe even repressed, discomforts of the earlier approach to Everest on foot. The comforting ability of memory to simplify and selectively soften the hard edges of the past had allowed me to imagine for decades that I had swanned through here with ease. My senses now said to me clearly, probably not!, as I was forced to recall the terrific blisters that 12 days of walking to this point had generated in 1963; my new expedition boots were completely unbroken-in. Later on this trip it hit me forcefully that on this little Khumbu adventure I experienced again, as if they had been fast-forwarded, some of the significant features, emotional features, of the whole four-month 1963 experience: vague and unreal expectations, shock on encountering the ground-level reality, struggle with negative thoughts, accommodation to the situation, reduction to just putting one foot in front of the other, repeating little mantras like "slow step, short step, closer all the time," and "just keep going." Only a return to the scene of the crime was able to bring back these not-so-pretty memories.

The trail finally comes around a sharp corner and one is looking up at a natural amphitheater, heavily terraced to allow houses to be built and a few crops to be grown. We entered the village near a spring at the bottom of the amphitheater where five or six laughing and healthy-looking women were washing clothes exactly as their mothers had 35 years before, and climbed upward along paths lined with small shops offering goods undreamed of in the Namche I had last visited—Mars bars, Nike shoes, Danish beer, Chivas Regal whiskey, as well as the latest trekking equipment, all of course brought here on yaks or backs.

> 2/20: The views were great as we got higher, I might have had slight memories of some of them, but my focus was really on just keeping going, on survival. Rests more and more frequent, mental focus on left-right rhythm and trying to control negative thoughts, such as, I hate this, I said I'd never do it again, I'm not sure I can make it, and, the little return I'm likely to get isn't worth it. Tried to focus on, This is the last uphill hiking of my life, only 2 hrs to Namche, etc., but it just got harder and harder. Good view of Everest at about 11. Edge of Namche at 12, but it still took more than half an hour to get to Panorama Lodge, at top of village. Resting every 10-15 steps. Village looks entirely new, stone, blue framing, looks prosperous as hell. Lots of beautiful Sherpa people around, doing laundry in central area, carding sweaters on the street, etc. Sherap knows most everybody. Little encounters ALL involve joking, ready laughter.

At 11,101 feet Namche is the lowest of the Khumbu Sherpa villages and probably the best known, though not the largest. In 1957, when the first anthropological fieldwork here was done, there were 73 households with a population of something like 400. Today I'd estimate the numbers to be nearly twice those [In the 2001 census the population was 1,647]. The houses in 1963 were mainly two-storied, the first for the animals and for feed and wood and the second for living. The houses today, which usually provide rooms or dormitories for tourists, are larger and more substantially built, with up to five stories, with tin rather than slate roofs, and with trim and roofs usually painted a vibrant color of blue. There were no tin roofs and hardly any color here in 1963. The whole impression is one of relative prosperity, and combined with Sherpa hospitality it makes an even more agreeable place than I remembered.

Namche Bazar

The Panorama Lodge, where I was staying, was near the top of the amphitheater. Having just come off that killer trail, it was all I could do to haul myself up there. Sherap was patient, telling me I was doing fine (I think he started to add "for your age" and then thought better of it—it's tricky dealing with these Westerners). After some soup and beer he told me about himself.

He was born in Namche, as were his father and grandfather, sometime in the 1950s. His father was hired on the famous 1953 British expedition that put Hillary on the summit of Everest, and carried loads as high as the South Col (about 26,000 feet). But he became ill there, and later decided expedition work was not his cup of tea; Everest was his first and his last outing. He then took two wives concurrently (so one could not say he wasn't ambitious) and the three adults lived together, eventually producing 13 children of which Sherap was one of the first. Having turned his back on carrying for climbers, the father went into trading and spent a lot of time in Tibet, apparently leaving the rest of the family in Namche most of the time. In 1959 he was in Lhasa when the Chinese invaded in force; he and other Sherpa traders hid in the Potala [Now a museum, the Potala used to be the winter palace of the Dalai Lama], but the Chinese found them and even though the Sherpas carried valid Nepalese passports the Chinese put them in jail and burned the passports. Sherap's father remained in jail in Lhasa for three years.

Meanwhile Sherap's mother got in touch with the Nepalese Foreign Ministry who agreed to help her get her husband's release. The Chinese authorities in Lhasa however claimed they couldn't locate Sherap's father. In the end his mother undertook the long and difficult trail to Lhasa herself, actually found him, and with the help of the Nepalese Embassy was able to get him out of prison. I presume the children stayed in Namche with the second wife.

It seems the father and mother stayed on in Lhasa for another seven years, carrying on some kind of business, with only occasional visits to Khumbu. By 1969 the business was not doing well and the parents returned to Namche, where the whole large family was reunited. Sherap at this point was attending the Hillary school in Khumjung and must have been in his teens. The arrangement of three adults and 13 children in one house did not work out, and in 1970 the family split; Sherap's mother and her eight children stayed in the house, the father, his second wife, and their five children moved to another house in Namche.

With the split, Sherap had to leave school and start helping to support his mother and siblings. In 1970 he served as porter on an expedition, and then was offered a job at the newly built Japanese Everest View Hotel, which sits a bit above Namche. He was given some training as a waiter as well as some advanced training in English (which he had already studied in Khumjung), and worked there for nearly two years. But this indoor job was unsatisfying for him and he was restless to do something else.

His entry into the trekking business, which was just then starting to mushroom, came through a Namche Sherpa called Pasang Kami, better known and in fact well-known as PK, about whom I'll have more to say later (he had been a mail-runner for us in 1963). In 1972 PK was working for Jimmy Roberts' Mountain Travel, and Sherap was able through PK to get work with Mountain Travel himself. In the autumn of 1972 he started working with trekking parties, and in the spring of 1973 he was assigned to be a cookboy or kitchen helper on an Italian expedition to Everest. This turned out to be the largest expedition ever mounted on Everest (and possibly anywhere!): 64 climbers, 120 Sherpas, 3000 porter loads—and I had never even heard of it!

Sherap went higher on Everest than he had expected, but it had nothing to do with his mountaineering ability. One of the wealthy backers of this almost incredibly massive effort was among the crowd staying at Base Camp, where Sherap was supposed to work. Unfortunately for Sherap the man had eyes for him. To get out of the situation Sherap had to get higher than the pursuer was able to go so he persuaded his sirdar to move him up to camp 2, above 21,000 feet, even though the insurance (which expeditions have to carry on Sherpas) did not cover him to that altitude. Italian hormones are apparently undaunted at least up to 18,000 feet; how much higher we cannot say since the experiment was terminated there by Sherap's intransigence.

Since that spring Sherap has continued to work for Mountain Travel, as guide and as sirdar on trekking expeditions throughout Nepal. He has had his share of sponsors. In 1980 some American climbers came through as trekkers, and afterwards invited him back to California to take an intensive course in climbing techniques. He did that, at their expense, and told me that his month's climbing and trekking in the Sierras was one of the best times of his life. Apparently he hoped that it would give him the opportunity to be hired as sirdar on mountaineering expeditions when he returned. But his absence had given his wife time to think about it, and she greeted him with a clear No Climbing message. He's learned to live with that but I think it hasn't been easy.

Around 1987 he was befriended by some German trekking clients, who gave him a loan enabling him to start building his lodge. So Sherap has been able to ride the wave of tourist interest in the Khumbu in a fairly comfortable manner. His two children are now in school in Kathmandu, and the older one, a boy, is hoping to attend the University of Colorado in the fall of 1998. Last year Sherap and his wife visited friends in Germany for three months, hoping it might turn up some employment there (it didn't), and when we parted days later he let me know that he'd be interested to work in the United States for at least a summer, which is the monsoon season in Nepal and a time of inactivity in Namche. I think Sherap is restless again.

———

My second day in Namche was market day. I spent half the wet and chilly morning milling about in a crowd of Sherpas, of course, but also Rais, Tamangs, and other tribes I can't identify. And Tibetans, some of whom would have come from four or five days away to sell their goods, the most prominent of which were huge chunks of dried meat. Travelers since the last century have been struck with the "ferocious" aspect of Tibetans (a far cry from their presentation in recent movies), and these were true to form—dirty clothes, greasy hair, deeply tanned and wrinkled skin, some wearing red bandanas in their hair which are supposed to signal the warrior class. All this is absolutely wiped away when you see them smile their stunning smiles.

Market traders in Namche

By mid-morning I felt it was time to get down to business. A reconnaissance arranged for me by Jimmy Roberts before he died led me to believe there were some 16 Sherpas still around who had been with us. I found the first four here in Namche.

The first was Kancha, who was born in Namche around 1933. The story of his life that he gave me, sitting in the small trekker's lodge that he now owns, made him sound almost a perfect illustration of the changes in Sherpa life. His father, also Namche-born, was a trader and small businessman, so Kancha's early memories are of the trips to Tibet. There were of course no schools at this time to keep him off these trading treks. As he described those days, food was hard to come by and almost everything, including the wool for their clothes, had to be obtained by barter and brought back to the village. He recalled carrying loads of rice-paper from Nepal to Tibet, where the monasteries needed them for copying religious documents, and heavy loads of salt back to Nepal. They also brought back wool, some of which his mother wove into rugs which they then sold to the farmers lower down. These trading expeditions were organized by the wealthier men in Khumbu, so Kancha's father and family were not operating as entrepreneurs but as hired help, and Kancha recalled that for carrying one load from Namche to Tibet his father was paid five rupees. He particularly remembered continually being sent into the woods to bring back firewood, both at home and on the trail.

When he was 18 or 19, probably in 1952, he ran away to Darjeeling with two other young boys. Having stolen a little money and food from their parents, the boys left at night and hiked almost without stopping for three days, fearing all the while that someone would come after them to drag them home. But the escape was a success, and once in Darjeeling Kancha went to Tenzing.

> I looking Tenzing, Tenzing's house, and I find Tenzing's house, and Tenzing: Who are you? Whose son? he asked me. Then my father name I give to him, Whoo! My good friend, your father my good friend! Come, come, my house! I worked four months his house, and some bring wood and washing things, I worked there. You stay there, my house, and I take you to Everest. I very happy!

So Kancha, through Tenzing, got his first job as sherpa on the 1953 British expedition, where he carried loads as high as the South Col (26,000 feet). He laughed, remembering that in 1953 there was no paper money, only coins, and the pay destined for porters and Sherpas had to be carried in five large boxes, with five Sherpas to guard them. At the end of the expedition, Kancha said, Hillary and Tenzing flew back to Kathmandu in a helicopter (rare in Nepal at that time), and after that, he said, "Tenzing like king. We never saw!"

Apparently Kancha's next expedition was with us in 1963, where he worked largely as an assistant on the glaciology research project with Dr. Maynard Miller. It was ironic that Kancha should have probably his first contact with technology in this wild setting. Miller had a device that took seismographic readings, which required Kancha to hit a metal plate sitting on the ice with a hammer, and the results were printed on a piece of paper as a graph. Sherap paraphrased for me that "the more he hits harder and harder, the picture is better." This made both Kancha and Sherap laugh loudly.

After AMEE, Kancha went back to trading with Tibet, but now dealing more in luxury items such as watches. He said the Chinese soldiers he dealt with loved the watches he brought over, but he was trading illegally and at some point Chinese government authorities confiscated his whole inventory, and he lost everything. In fact, when I asked him what was the worst thing he could recall in his life, this was it.

Having worked under Jimmy Roberts in 1963 Kancha then became one of Mountain Travel's early guides, and this was his salvation after the loss in Tibet. From that low point he worked his way back to a comfortable position in life, starting with Mountain Travel (13 years), then with Himalayan Journeys, and finally with Malla Trek. When I asked Kancha who had been the most important person in his life, he replied that Tenzing had been very important but that really it was Jimmy Roberts, since he first hired him and taught him the skills on which he built his career. Somewhere along the way he put together the money for a lodge as well, which together with his small pension is his living today. He retired from trekking two years ago, at 63.

Kancha had two sons and two daughters. At least three of these have been involved in the trekking business. As a guide one of the daughters attracted a Danish client, whom she married, and she now lives in Denmark. Kancha has never visited Denmark, which surprised me and I asked why? "No necessary (laughs). No lama, no monastery. We like the lama, monastery (laughs). They have two sons, bring two, three time here." One of the sons now lives in Chicago, another place Kancha has never visited.

Kancha looked healthy and mellow. I had heard from another source that he had struggled for a while with an alcohol addiction but he has conquered that through a heavy investment in religious devotion. I asked him if he was happy in his retirement. "Very happy now. Because my son, everybody's married, go away, my older son go [to Chicago], and then the second son, he stay this house. Everybody married, two daughter married." The youngest son, in Sherpa tradition, is the one who inherits house and land, and Kancha is glad he has a son to pass it on to – and probably even more glad that he has something to pass on.

> 2/21: I'm connecting with what I'm doing now, feel much better, see value in the interviews, fun to watch the people being interviewed (and the family watch us). These interviews are a sort of minor event here, brings a little attention to these older guys who are mostly just hanging around.

Sherap and I left Kancha, intending to return to the Panorama Lodge for lunch. On the way we had to move off the narrow trail to make room for several yaks and a Sherpa. The man turned out to be Pasang Tendi, one of the class of '63 whom I didn't expect to find in Namche. We seized the moment and went into his Namche house (he has another in Khumjung) for an interview.

Pasang Tendi was 18 in 1963, and so still only 53 when we met on the trail. His grandparents were born in Tibet, his parents in Khumjung. Until 1963 he lived the conventional life in Khumbu, helping his father farm and care for their yaks, but all the while with expeditions on his mind. He heard about the American expedition to be formed in Kathmandu, and made his way there where he managed to be hired as one of our 900+ porters. This was what he had hoped for, had gone there for. It seems that as far as Thyangboche Monastery, the next day's stop after Namche, he served as Jimmy Roberts' personal porter. For some unknown reason, perhaps related to the fact that Pasang's older brother Ang Tsering was already on board as a sherpa, at Thyangboche Jimmy changed Pasang's status from porter to sherpa, meaning that he would stay with the expedition when the porters were dismissed and participate in the climb. It was a big jump for Pasang who thought he would have to porter for several years before he could qualify as sherpa.

Once above Base Camp Pasang was assigned, beyond the general load-carrying that all Sherpas did, as personal sherpa for Tom Hornbein and Willi Unsoeld, who were two of the more remarkable climbers on the team. He carried at least one load to the South Col, and then became one of the support team for Tom and Willi's attempt on the unclimbed West Ridge. At one point, in preparation for the summit attempt, Pasang was with a small group of Sherpas camped above Advance Base (21,500 feet) on the West Ridge route, when an avalanche caught them by complete surprise. Hornbein wrote in his diary:

> To add to the excitement and to our difficulties, yesterday four Sherpas cooking tea [Pasang told me they actually were in the middle of a card game] in the tents at the Dump were suddenly accosted by a powder-snow avalanche. It carried them several hundred feet downhill, rolling them up in the tents, and providing a nice ride down [a typical bit of Hornbein humor here]. Their axes, crampons, and ropes, sitting outside, were lost. They came down to Advance Base without them, but able to laugh at the whole episode. ... All four kept their good humor as they descended to Base Camp for rest, but only Pasang Tendi volunteered to go up on the West Ridge again. (p. 122)

Pasang was back on the West Ridge a few days later when Hornbein and Unsoeld got their spectacular ascent and traverse of the summit under way. Pasang and four other Sherpas carried loads to a high point of 27,250 feet; from there Tom and Willi were on their own. Ullman wrote only what everyone knew:

> No one knew better than Willi Unsoeld and Tom Hornbein, taking their leave from them [the five Sherpas], that if it had not been for what these, their companions, had done that day [carrying loads so high], there would have been no tomorrow—whatever the outcome. (p 242)

I asked Pasang whether he had liked being on Everest and Sherap gave me his reply: "Yes, he said, he did. He was young and he was strong, and he really liked it."

Pasang went to Everest again as a climbing sherpa with an Indian expedition in the middle 1960s, and carried loads to the highest camp. The Indian member with whom he was paired on that trip asked him back on the International Everest Expedition of 1971. Pasang joined, but while he was still at Base Camp his wife hiked up from Khumjung (several days walk up to 18,000 feet) and demanded that he leave the expedition. That put an end to Pasang's climbing. Any arguments he might have made later were probably silenced by the fact that the Indian member with whom he would have been climbing was killed on this expedition.

Since then I gather he has supported himself mainly in the traditional way, through farming and managing a herd of cattle, although Sherap told me he has in fact been on other expeditions but only as cook or in some other base camp role. Pasang Tendi has another brother, Pertemba, who has been a highly valued sherpa on many expeditions, and I wish I had explored with Pasang how hard it has been for him to see his brother doing what he wanted to do.

Pasang Tendi, who carried loads as high as 27,250 feet for the 1963 West Ridge summit attempt, Namche

---

2/21: At some meal or other, Sherap added chili powder, which was usually offered and he always took. Told me they call it "Sherpa oxygen" -- it's what they need to keep going.

Sherap and I had made an appointment to see PK (Pasang Kami), and after lunch it was time to move on again. PK owns and runs the largest lodge in Namche Bazar, and may be in certain ways the most important man in the village. I had been warned that it was hard to get and to hold his attention, as it turned out to be, but he did make himself available for our appointment. We sat in the kitchen at his lodge. At 3 in the afternoon his dining room was full and we were in the midst of high-energy activity in the kitchen, with frequent interruptions as PK answered questions, barked directions, and hailed people going in and out.

PK was born around 1939, to parents who had come to the Khumbu from Tibet. His father was a farmer and trader and of course the whole family participated. In the chaotic course of this interview I got very little information about his early life, but I know that by 1957 he was working as a porter for local traders, and did not go out on his first expedition until 1960. His first trip to Everest was with an Indian group in 1962.

He must have been about 24 when he was recruited by Jimmy Roberts to join AMEE. Jimmy had often been in the Khumbu region, hunting and exploring, and he knew the group with whom PK ran: "Some guys, Ang Tsering from Khumjung, knew him. Also, he coming, doing some research, Jimmy and, those people you know, Shipton and Tilman, they worked together with Jimmy."

Eric Shipton and H. W. Tilman are two of the most famous British climbers and explorers of the Himalayas. The visits PK refers to must have been in the 1950s, although both of them had been to the Himalayas via Tibet before that.

PK was hired on to AMEE as a mail-runner, what you might call an entry-level job, in spite of his prior experience on Everest. He was one of two, and their job was to shuttle between Base Camp and Kathmandu carrying dispatches and mail. He told me they could make the one-way trip to Kathmandu in five days—they must have trotted the whole way! And the other mail-runner, Palden, was nearly 60 at the time! On one occasion PK got as far as Namche and found a helicopter had just delivered someone there, and was able to hitch a ride the rest of the way to Kathmandu on the return flight. Or so he thought; unfortunately the plane developed engine trouble and crash-landed about halfway back to Kathmandu. No one was hurt, and PK managed to shave a little time off his trip, but the pilot ended up being stuck in the village of Jiri for weeks waiting for a spare part, while PK and Palden ran back and forth.

PK's own rambling account of his expedition history was brief but suggests he was ambitious. He went with a British expedition to western Nepal in the autumn of '63, just months after Everest, and in the spring of '64 was part of Erwin Schneider's cartographical expedition. In the years 1955-57 Schneider had produced by far the best map of the Nepalese side of the Everest region to that time, using five Sherpas in support. The 1964 effort was aimed at extending that map; to accomplish it PK and 30 other Sherpas were in the field for six months. This was more like the early days of British surveying:

> No trail, just pushing the bamboo, waterfalls, bare foot, you know, crossing. We are catching the heights, the measurements, the map, you know. Six months. We had 5 rupees per day, salary. And we had something like 31 Sherpas. We split the group into different areas. We had to walk, trek, in the morning with the bare feet, and that was October. (JL: Why bare feet?) Because the stream, there's no bridge, you have to take off the shoes and then all those little rocks touching your feet, got a bit cold, you know. Hard life, I never had such a hard life.

This too-short vignette is misleading. In fact at one point Schneider's group went nine days without food and they ended up eating washed and boiled leather before they found a friendly village. I'm sure that PK's last sentence above is no over-statement.

PK has been with the Indians three more times, with several German and with at least one Japanese expedition. In the spring of 1970 he went as sirdar with a now-famous British expedition, led by Chris Bonington, which climbed the south face of Annapurna. PK was a last-minute replacement for Ang Temba, "a seasoned high-altitude porter of the old school", whose wife had known so many Sherpas hurt or killed in recent years that she forbade him to go out again. Bonington wrote in his account, "I suspect we benefited from the change; although Pasang later had some trouble with his health, his administrative ability amply made up for this."

He spoke a fluent, pedantically correct English, addressed me and everyone else on the expedition as an equal [the British were not yet quite ready for this development], yet got on with the job of organizing the day-to-day management of the party, chasing up the whereabouts of stray loads or any odd items that were wanted by members of the expedition. In appearance he reminded me of a very 'with-it' French guide, for he was always immaculately dressed and wore the white peaked cap much favoured by the Corps of Chamonix Guides. He was quite slightly built and has much finer features than the average Sherpa. He was very much more sophisticated than the high-altitude Sherpas I had known on my two previous expeditions, who had spoken very limited English and were essentially simple villagers. ... I think Pasang probably represents the start of a new breed of Sherpa, partly spawned by their changing role in Nepal, where the bulk of their work is confined to conducting parties of tourists on treks round the valleys. The ideal qualifications for this job are organizing ability, command of languages and a good manner. Pasang had cultivated all three, although his background was the same as that of the traditional Sherpa. (pp. 43-45)

Suddenly PK's success as hotelier and rise to prominence in Namche doesn't seem surprising anymore. His last expedition was the American Bicentennial in 1976. He spent some 18 years guiding trekkers for Mountain Travel, and then, with two other Sherpas, (including Pasang Tendi's brother, Pertemba) opened his own trekking company, Nepal Himal Trekking; they have been quite successful with it.

From what Bonington wrote it's clear that if any Sherpa were going to attract a sponsor it would be PK. In 1985 he served as sirdar for a trekking group organized by ex-President Jimmy Carter and his wife. He was well-liked and although I don't know what benefits flowed to him from that I suspect it may have helped make the building of his lodge possible. Another pair of clients of substance (what the British used to call "the quality") were Dick Blum and Diane Feinstein, the one-time mayor of San Francisco. PK now owns the key to that city and has visited several times. Blum is a man of considerable financial resources, and as a result of his trekking experiences he set up the American Himalayan Foundation. In the 1997 fund-raising brochure Blum wrote:

> Those of us who first came to this magnificent part of the world for the challenge of the mountains have been deeply touched by the people who call the top of the world their home. They have simple material requirements, but it is clear to all who visit that their need for medical, educational and environmental assistance is great. Sherpas, Nepalis and Tibetans, living in poverty in the remote regions of the Himalayas have better lives because of your compassion.

The Foundation operates through a number of existing agencies and aid efforts, all of them admirable but so many that I can't help wondering whether it is spreading itself too thin. To some extent the Foundation might be considered as an unintended consequence of PK's now undeniable charm. Incidentally, one of the Foundation's accomplishments has been a dental clinic in Namche, currently staffed by two Canadian-trained dental technicians, one of whom is PK's daughter.

When we left PK I commented to Sherap about the second mail-runner, who apparently had been able to match PK's pace at more than twice his age. "Oh, would you like to meet him?" he asked. It turns out that Palden is still alive and living with his wife in Namche. He is reputed to be 93 and many believe he is the oldest man in Khumbu. He is popular with villagers who love to visit with him, share his stories, bring him news and occasional gifts of money. Apparently a gift of the local alcoholic beverage, *rakshi,* is especially appreciated and I was very sorry I had none to offer. The interview was short but I learned that he too had gone to Darjeeling in his youth and had been engaged on several early expeditions, although he remembered few details. But after several of his friends were killed while climbing, Palden took only such jobs as mail-runner or kitchen-boy and went no higher than base camp. The strategy worked well, since he's still around to talk about it.

———

Above the terraces of Namche Bazar the slope of the hillside levels out a bit. There is a fairly flat section near the edge of the gorge strewn with huge boulders and called Jarok (which means "boulder"), and in among these Sherap and I found the small house that belongs to Dawa Tenzing. Da, as anyone named Dawa seems to be called, was my personal sherpa on AMEE and I was especially interested to find out what he had been doing. We had no way of communicating in 1963 and much of the time we were not staying in the same camp, so there was no closeness. All the same he "looked after" me, perhaps considering me his burden (I always wondered about this since he never looked particularly happy the way so many of the Sherpas do so much of the time).

Da Tenzing was born the same year as Kancha, 1933, so he was 30 at the time of AMEE and 65 when I interviewed him. His memory seemed cloudier than any of the others, he frequently consulted his wife about questions I asked, and the information I got was unhappily thin. We did establish that he was born and raised in Namche, and I believe he never left for Darjeeling or even Kathmandu in search of expedition work. Nevertheless it came his way. In 1955 he was on the Swiss expedition to Lhotse, the fourth highest of the world's mountains and a peak that adjoins Everest. The leader of that expedition was Norman Dyhrenfurth, the organizer of AMEE, and the sirdar was Da's wife's uncle, Pasang Phutar, who was later recruited as sirdar for AMEE. So Da was well-connected by the time

AMEE sherpas were being hired. Also, it appears that Da was another of the 31 Sherpas who worked for Irwin Schneider's difficult mapping expedition in the middle 1950s, and that must have been a strong recommendation in his favor. And finally, he was a climbing sherpa on the very nearly successful 1962 Indian Everest expedition and carried to the Indians' highest camp.

On AMEE, Da Tenzing's load-carrying was mostly on the South Col route, where he was seen as strong and reliable. He was one of the porters who carried loads to the highest camp at nearly 28,000 feet. At the beginning of the final push to the summit by Whittaker and Gombu, Dyhrenfurth and Ang Dawa and four Sherpas (including Dawa Tenzing) formed their support team. At 26,000 feet Norman discovered his oxygen equipment was leaking; the Sherpas were asked for a volunteer to exchange units with him but all refused. Ang Dawa insisted on trading units with Norman. On the following day, when Norman and Ang Dawa were to head up to 28,000 feet, Norman demanded that one of the Sherpas give up his equipment to Ang Dawa and a man named Ang Nyima did so. However, the next day he talked Ang Dawa into taking it back. This left Ang Dawa again headed for the summit with defective oxygen equipment. The summit team had expected the four Sherpas who were now to depart for a lower camp to leave their partially used tanks and descend without oxygen.

> But when the time came the Sherpas were having none of it. ... On the Swiss expedition of 1956, they pointed out, the porters had gone down from the highest camp using oxygen—and if this was all right for the Swiss, why not with the Americans? Jim and Gombu did their futile best to persuade them. When they saw it was a lost cause, they pleaded that at least one set with a good regulator be left, so that Ang Dawa would not have to climb the next day with a leaking valve. And at last, as on the previous night at the Col, one hero emerged: this time the Sherpa Dawa Tenzing. (p. 179)

Da Tenzing still remembered this episode and reminded me of it, via Sherap: "He didn't use his oxygen, because Ang Dawa's regulator didn't work. So he gave his regulator to Ang Dawa, and he didn't use much oxygen, he didn't use that much. Norman liked him very much about that."

After Whittaker and Gombu had reached the summit by the Hillary route, Da was switched to the West Ridge. Hornbein referred to him briefly:

> The Sherpas were tired. Many had carried to the South Col twice and several had been to Camp 6. Whether they were physically drained or whether they figured that now the mountain was climbed it was foolish to ask for more trouble, I don't know. Phu Dorje and Dawa Tenzing, two of the strong men on the Col route, turned back from the carry that Willi took to 4W. Before their lack of enthusiasm could infect the others, I sent them on down to Advance Base. Illness and inertia ran rampant, but were cured in part by Jimmy Roberts' voice over the radio promising extra pay ... Our progress held to schedule.

In 1971 Da climbed with a Japanese expedition, but that was his last climb. After that he appears to have joined other expeditions but only as cook and never going above base camp. I got the impression that Da Tenzing wanted a traditional Sherpa life, and expeditions were only a way to get money to buy a house and cattle. He told me that the best thing in his life was the day in 1969 when he was able to buy his house in Jarok. The worst thing had been an unusually harsh winter when he lost most of his precious herd of yaks and had to start all over again.

Dawa Tenzing and his wife have six children, two boys and four girls. The older boy is married and living in Namche, probably working in the tourist industry. Two of the girls are married, living in Kathmandu, and connected with the trekking business. The youngest boy, only 14, is in school and living at home. He was too shy to answer my question about what he wanted to do, but after a vigorous exchange between Da and his wife Sherap summarized for me: "Dawa Tenzing says, I have nothing, no big hopes. I will just give him a good education until he -- far as he goes. Whatever he does, it's his choice."

Dawa Tenzing with his house and son, Jarok

KHUMJUNG AND KUNDE

Leaving Jarok, Sherap and I hiked up a trail now lined with small boulders; they were much more abundant here than below Namche. We passed mothers and children, both carrying wicker baskets supported by a tump line over their heads, sometimes filled with vegetables but most often with rocks; I suppose they had been clearing a field. We passed men leading yaks (and naks and zopkios, both variants of yaks) to or from the higher-altitude pastures, and at about 12,500 feet we crossed over the airstrip at Syangboche, built on the same plan as Lukla's but seldom-used, and then mainly by chartered helicopters bringing one- or two-night visitors to the Everest View Hotel. Beyond that we crested the ridge at about 13,000 feet and headed down the other side to the twin villages of Khumjung and Kunde. The trail was well-worn from daily use by young scholars from Namche getting to and from the school in Khumjung. It was also deeply muddy and very slippery from recent rain; Sherap and I held hands a lot.

Rocks everywhere, as far as the eye could see! Rock walls lined both sides of every path crisscrossing Khumjung, leading up to Kunde, and away to the monastery at Thyangboche. Lower down I had been bowled over by imagining the effort that had to go into the terracing of steep hillsides for farming; here I felt the same, imagining the work of moving and placing this multitude of rocks. The village is on flatter ground than is Namche (every village is!) and has a more spacious feel, the more so as you can look to the north and see the monastery at Thyangboche sitting on a distant ridge, with the sheer snow-covered walls of Ama Dablam (22,494 feet) looming behind it.

We entered the village through a portal carrying Buddhist inscriptions and fine paintings of Buddhist scenes, which Sherap explained had been paid for and placed there by the family in memory of one of our Sherpas, Ang Tsering. Before AMEE Ang Tsering had worked with the British in 1953, and at the tender age of 15 or 16 had carried loads as high as the South Col. The team had wanted him to help carry equipment back to Kathmandu after the climb, but there was resistance to overcome.

> ...Tenzing had stayed on at the Thyangboche camp site to bring on the loads left there unclaimed. Soon he appeared himself, in happy mood from the celebrations, accompanied by Ang Tsering bearing a carpet. This, it appeared later, was a subterfuge. Ang Tsering also had been forbidden by his mother to accompany the expedition, for fear that he might be corrupted by the glittering pleasures of the wicked capital. But she yielded so far as to allow him to carry for Tenzing the first stage. Arriving at Tate that night Ang Tsering said, "Bother her," [an Anglicism which I very much doubt he ever uttered] and came the whole way. Arriving at Kathmandu, and perhaps fearing the maternal rod, he decided to accompany his companions to Darjeeling... (Noyce, p 221).

A source other than Sherap told me that in the late '60s and early '70s, while still young, he had become wealthy working as a contractor on the building of the Everest View Hotel. He was obviously very well respected in the village, and had been mayor of

Khumjung for a while. Of his five children the eldest son, Nima Wongchu, is a fine example of the leap many of the children of the class of '63 have made into the modern world. Nima got his secondary schooling on a scholarship from the American Himalayan Foundation. He went on to college in New Zealand, with help from the Foundation and also from the government of New Zealand, taking a degree in Forestry. He then brought his knowledge back to Nepal and worked in the government's National Park system for several years, before going to the United States for a Master's Degree at the University of Montana. He is now Chief Warden of Sagarmatha National Park, created to enforce and encourage conservation in the Everest region, with headquarters not far above the Panorama Lodge in Namche.

There is a younger son, Rinchen Karma, who works for Asian Airlines in Lukla, and three daughters. Tsering Doku is married to a Sherpa who runs a trekking agency in Kathmandu. Phurba Sonam, a beautiful woman whom I was privileged to meet in Kathmandu, is married to a Sherpa who is head of the Regional Office of the World Wildlife Fund. His job has given them a fair experience of the rest of the world, including two years living in Arlington, Virginia. (I learned nothing of the third daughter). I doubt any of us would have predicted such lives for the next generation back in 1963.

After 1963 Ang Tsering worked for Jimmy Roberts on several more expeditions until his wife asked him to stop. After that he worked many years for Hillary's organization helping to build schools and bridges. He died at the early age of 48, not from overwork (although his wife said that Hillary's sirdar worked his Sherpas very hard), but more likely from alcohol abuse. The story of his dying, as Sherap interpreted it for me, is colorful and gives some more clues to Sherpa life:

> For Sherpas, always every 12 years is a bad year. Even the Thyangboche lamas said, OK, don't send him any far—keep him home, 48 is quite dangerous. So they were always here. And her first son,

Nima Wongchu, came back after two years serving in Langtang National Park. He came, and he was so happy to see his son, after two years, you know, so they were drinking wildly. And one night he was just so, he was unconscious, he was unconscious and she was so [upset], she called Pasang Tendi, he was neighbor and brother, too. So all night they stayed, and in that morning, he woke and everybody said, OK, you were like this, and so Pasang Tendi say him, No more drinking. No more drinks. So he agreed that he will never drink again. At that time Pertemba was on an expedition, and Pasang Tendi and Ang Tsering were supposed to pick up another trekking group, support group, from Lukla, they were supposed to go to Lukla, and Ang Tsering said, OK, I can't come today, I will come tomorrow, I will catch up you tomorrow. Why don't you take my zopkio and [everything] today. So Pasang Tendi and Kami left. And he was fine that morning, and about afternoon the next day, you know, that day, afternoon, he was shaking. He didn't drink any alcohol, anything, he was, very shaking. Nima went to call the doctor, and some other religious men, they went for lama, she [his wife] wanted both. Doctor came and doctor said he didn't have any blood, he was low blood, he needed the (glucose?) thing. She said, Well, today is bad day. We can't send him to hospital or any out of house, has to stay house. So the doctor ran up to the hospital, to bring some medicine. And by the time doctor got here he had died. ...In the morning he [Ang Tsering] had apologized for drinking too much, said he would never drink again, but it was too late.

Sherap had arranged that we stay with Ang Tsering's elegant widow, Doma Chhamsi, who lives in a spacious house (not a lodge) where I was given a large family room finely paneled in dark wood and with wall-to-ceiling glass-doored cupboards on two walls. It was the most affluence I saw in Khumbu, though I now suspect there are many other rich interiors hiding behind fairly conventional exteriors. I was baffled by the enormous locks I found on most of the doors of the house, both outside and inside, until I realized that the house sat empty for a good part of every winter, which she spends with her daughter in Kathmandu. (Of the rooms I saw only the kitchen had any source of heat.) She, incidentally, had carried loads as a porter for the British in 1953; looking at her aristocratic bearing today I had trouble picturing her as a 12-year-old girl with a tump line over her head and a box on her back.

Doma Chhamsi, the widow of Ang Tsering, Kunde

Late in the afternoon Sherap and I were sitting in the kitchen having tea when a small, wiry man materialized in the room, as if out of thin air, and I was introduced to Nawang Dorje. He was one of two of our Sherpas whom I knew to be still living in Khumjung so I was delighted to have him simply appear like this. My delight climbed higher and higher during the next few hours as Nawang Dorje showed himself to be a magnificent story-teller. It took almost nothing to get him started and only the occasional shot of whiskey to keep him going. He spoke only in Sherpa and I had to rely entirely on

Sherap's summaries and explanations, but Nawang's body language and voice inflections captivated my attention and I was often belly-laughing before I even knew what he had said. He was a master. After a little while he was joined by the other man I was looking for, Pemba Tenzing, who played straight man to Nawang's performance. Sitting on a window-seat looking exactly like Chairman Mao, Pemba giggled almost continuously and led the outright laughter at many points.

> 2/22: Good synergy within group, fantastic good feeling, much laughter. Try to picture: Sherap and I sitting against one wall, burner in front, widow and Tamang servant flitting in and out, black puppy in and out, little boy comes and sits in corner, quiet as mouse, wide-eyed, watching each of us. Stories back and forth.

Nawang was born probably around 1931, since he claims to be 67 now. His father had a lot of cattle and taking care of them ("like a cowboy," he said) is mainly what Nawang remembers from his childhood. In his early twenties, possibly in 1953 (but no dates in this story seemed certain), he made what will by now be familiar to the reader as the Great Escape, to Darjeeling. Sherap paraphrased his telling of this, which had been punctuated with lots of laughter:

> It's a long story. Well, first he planned to escape, so he tried to take, get some food. So he took about five kilos of tsampa, put it into a sack, and he wanted to hide it. So, in a field there was a big hole, you know, after they dig out potatoes, they store them in there, so he thought it might be the best place to hide [the tsampa]. But in the morning, some rat came, turned it out, [spread it] all over. So his father saw that, oh, he was so mad at him! So finally he promised him, OK, I will not go, I will not try to escape again. It was very hard life, you know, without shoes, he had to go always with yak. So one time, his father came from Lukla, bringing some small

yak. So before the last village before Namche, there he had some load of food, wheat, about 40 kilos of wheat, he left it there, he couldn't carry on. So he came back, and he said [to Nawang], OK, you go back and get those kilos. Well, of course, his father trusted him that he won't escape, he promised that. So he goes back, and on the trail a guy from Jarok was carrying about 40-50 kilos of salt, rock salt, go down below and sell it. And bring back some food. So, they talked, you know, about escaping, so he said, OK, why not? We go there! We'll sell this salt, we'll go. So they... sold the salt, and the food his father left and also a really nice tea-cup of his father's was in the sack, he sold that. So what he got was 70 rupees, and the other guy got 120. And they headed for Darjeeling (laughter).

While Sherpa life in the days before tourism was very much organized around family ties, there was no sentimentality about it, none of the Hallmark-card kind of emotion. Every Sherpa I talked with who ran away in search of work in Darjeeling seems to have had no trouble taking whatever he needed from the family reserves, including even a prized tea-cup.

Nawang's adventures in Darjeeling, even after filtering through Sherap's brief summaries, had the feel of a Dickens story, a kind of Sherpa *Oliver Twist*. First he stayed with a female cousin, and worked on the building of a road into Sikkim. But his friend Pemba Tenzing (the one sitting with us enjoying Nawang's stories) was already in Darjeeling and living among a circle of Sherpa people, and Nawang was encouraged to move into the house of one of this circle. After a while the wife in this family told him they had a neighbor who might be able to get him an expedition job. So taking a gift of eggs Nawang went to seek his fortune, and indeed a job was offered—but at a price. Nawang was either to pay the man 100 Indian rupees or turn over to him all his expedition clothing afterwards. Nawang wanted the job and agreed, then returned to his household where he explained what had happened. The head of the household held an important job with the Darjeeling mountaineering school, and was very angry that his neighbor had demanded payment for getting him a job. He confronted the neighbor, who was then very angry that Nawang had told anyone about their deal, and in the general turmoil that followed Nawang decided it was time for another escape. He gave up his claim to the job and went back to his cousin's house.

Some time later he crossed paths with the young Nawang Gombu (who went to the summit in 1963). Nawang Dorje was still looking for something better than road-building and Gombu suggested he might want to join the British Army which was taking on new recruits just then. He was soon in training, part of which was fitness training done outdoors in a field. His cousin knew nothing about this new career move, but one morning she passed the exercise field and saw him there. I don't know why but she hated seeing him in the army and took it upon herself to get him out again (anthropologists agree that women have a lot of authority in Sherpa families, and I heard a fair amount of evidence for the proposition). This seemed unfortunate since obviously Nawang needed a job and he seemed happy with the army. But the cousin came through for him, by then introducing him to Ang Tharkay, who had been hired as sirdar for the upcoming 1955 expedition to Makalu, and Ang Tharkay signed on Nawang for his first expedition job (as he also signed on other several other men who later were with AMEE).

Nawang claimed to me that he had been on 18 expeditions in his life, though he was unable to list them specifically. In 1960 he reached the summit of Dhaulagiri (26,810 feet) without oxygen. He said that he didn't experience any great happiness when he reached the summit, but when he returned to Kathmandu with the team, a great fuss was made and then he felt very happy.

> ...when he came to Kathmandu it was a big issue, radio, newspaper, and everybody came to see him, and it was big—at that time, you know—he said, I don't know if I made money or not, but at that time he was so please, so happy, everybody came to meet him. And then second time, couple of years ago there was a, couple of years

there was a big ceremony in France, for the summitters of the 8000-meter [mountains]. Everybody was invited in Chamonix, in France. So at that time he was also invited. Very please, VERY—that was about 4 or 5 years ago, he was very happy (much laughter all around the group).

In 1962 he was on Everest with an Indian expedition, but since he was the personal sherpa to the leader who was not a candidate for a summit team, Nawang didn't get above the South Col (26,000 feet). In 1964 he was on his third outing to Everest, but this time he was assigned to the camera crew, and again he didn't go above the South Col. He did, remarkably, remain on the South Col for ten days, the first four without oxygen; there would have been more days without oxygen except that he began scrounging among the many discarded oxygen bottles there and came up with two full ones!

On AMEE Nawang Dorje carried loads twice to the South Col, and then was one of 8 Sherpas who carried supplies to the highest camp (Camp 6, at about 28,000 feet) for Whittaker and Gombu. He was back at Base Camp when the news came down that the summit had been reached; Hornbein wrote: "Nawang Dorje came to ask for fuel for celebration. Will gave him a bottle of Scotch, which Nawang accepted with a mischievous grin. Though the Sherpas appeared less excited about the success than we were, they weren't going to pass up an excuse for a party." (p. 121)

After a brief rest Nawang was assigned to the West Ridge route, and carried loads to a similar altitude there. He might well have carried higher, but it seems he was part of the group of members and Sherpas who experienced a strong storm at Camp 3W and who were blown, still inside their tent, some 150 feet down a narrow snow ridge. A deviation to either side would have meant a long and lethal fall. Hornbein was in a tent that stayed put; he described what he found when he emerged to see what had happened:

RETURN TO THE SCENE OF THE CLIMB

...we stepped out into the staggering blast of the wind. Our headlights lit the swath planed by the sliding tents. Only then did we begin to appreciate the power of the storm, and imagine the horror of suddenly waking to find your tent sliding across the snow, accelerating in a headlong journey toward Tibet. By some miracle the tents had stopped in a shallow depression just below. Like surrealistic sculpture, their external frames were now a mass of contorted tubing from which the skin flapped noisily....There was a certain fatalistic humor in the voices within. (pp. 136-7)

Sherap paraphrased Nawang's account of the slide:

...he was cooking, and suddenly there was a very strong wind, and it blew all the tents, he says about twice as far as that house [pointing out the window]. Wind blew them. They had always the air mattress, ... all the air mattress was up above, they were very lucky that the wind took them in a gully. It was safe for them. They were very lucky. Finally they got up and they had to come back down to camp 2, they were cancelled for the summit, the Sherpas were cancelled for the summit, so only two members went [Hornbein and Unsoeld].

Jimmy Roberts had come through Khumbu many times before 1963 as he meandered around Nepal. According to Nawang Dorje he, Ang Tsering (in whose house we were talking) and Pemba Rinzing were his favorites to carry for him on his wanderings. So Nawang had more stories about Jimmy than he was able to tell in our one session. He surprised me, for example, with the news that Col. Jimmy Roberts, to every indication a confirmed bachelor, had twice wanted to marry Sherpa girls. Sherap translated:

Chumbi was a very famous guy from Khumjung, his daughter was a nurse. ... So [Jimmy] asked them to arrange a marriage for him. ... Jimmy said, OK [see] if you can arrange this, my marriage with

Nima Yangji, Nima Yangji was the girl, the nurse. She said, NO! And another Sherpa girl, she was also very beautiful, her name is Ang Tamji, and they went to ask about her. And her mother was so pissed off! How can my daughter marry to him? They are not Buddhists, they have a different color (all laugh), different skin, no way! So both of them refused him.

Nawang told us about one of the trips he made with Jimmy, to reconnoiter a route, but not to climb, on Dhaulagiri IV. There were 8 Sherpas this time, including Nawang and his good friend Pemba Tenzing. This trip must have taken place some time in the 1950s. Apparently even at that late date the local villagers in the vicinity of the mountain had never seen a foreigner and they didn't like the looks of Jimmy Roberts. They refused to let him in and wouldn't sell food to them. So once again the Sherpas showed their talent for improvising. In Sherap's words:

> So they had to lie. They lied. They said they came from the government, to research in the villages what they needed for development. They need bridges, water, or everything (laughter). So, the best thing was, they always went to the village mayor's house. They said these things, and Jimmy stayed inside his tent. And Jimmy had the gun, he always took the gun for shooting, hunting gun. And Nawang always stood with the gun, like a guard, acting like a policeman, beside his tent (much laughter) and Jimmy was laughing in his tent, because they had to lie, you know, they had to [pretend to be] very high rank government people. Pemba was very nice talking man, so he was the guy who went around the village and, you know, got the food, so he made the friend and got the food. Otherwise they wouldn't sell anything. He was very nice talking.

Nawang's last expedition was with a Japanese group in 1970, but four or five years before that he had started as a trekking sirdar for

Jimmy Roberts' new company, Mountain Travel. Sherap reported that Nawang stayed with Jimmy for some 17 years, one of the longest times that any Sherpa worked for Jimmy as sirdar.

Nawang had five children, four girls and a boy. One of the girls is now living in Chicago, thanks to a trekking contact. The man she married worked for Mountain Travel, and once had as a client an executive from IBM; that episode ripened into a sponsorship relationship that brought him and his family to the U.S. Two more daughters are married and living in Khumbu, and a third is still at home but engaged to be married soon. Nothing was said of the son; I learned later that he has always been a problem and has now disappeared, abandoning both his parents and his wife and children. At this point Nawang has scant resources, and although you could never guess it from his fun-loving attitude I was told that some days he and his wife have barely enough to eat.

And what of Pemba Tenzing? He preferred egging on his friend, Nawang Dorje, over talking about himself, and when I tried to stir him up he protested that his stories were the same as Nawang's: "We were very good friends and I don't have that much different stories." He made his way to Darjeeling working for an uncle who made trading trips to that part of the world, but I got nothing from him about how he got onto his first expeditions. He carried well for us and was one of two Sherpas who carried loads to the highest camp on the Hillary route (27,450 feet) in support of the second summit climbers (Lute Jerstad and Barry Bishop), then waited on the South Col (26,200 feet) for their return. After 1963 he was on four expeditions to Makalu, and worked his final expedition in 1970 with the Japanese. This was an unlucky expedition on which a number of Sherpas died. I'm guessing that had something to do with the fact that in 1970 or '71 he gave up mountaineering and started working at the newly built Everest View Hotel. He's still there—not getting rich, like some of his more entrepreneurial colleagues, but he's certainly getting by in a reasonably comfortable fashion and enjoying life in an infectious way. The last I saw of him he was sitting beside a stove at Syangboche, with a small white dog in his lap, smiling his head off.

> 2/22: I felt so down at rest time, but this really revived me! To bed at 8:15, it's freezing in the big, beautiful room I was in. Photos on the wall include Sherpa family at Disneyland.

Kunde is a sort of suburb of Khumjung, smaller and a little higher up, but only a 20-minute hike away. As far as I knew none of our still-living Sherpas lived there, but I had some hope of finding a relative or two. So Sherap and I continued foraging. Some, we found, had gone to the higher pastures with their cattle, but we did find and enjoy the hospitality of the oldest sister of one of our better sherpas, Girmi Dorje, who had died on a mountain in 1973.

Urken Doma, Girmi's sister, told me that her parents were Tibetan and that she, their first child, had been born in Tibet. She wasn't clear about when they migrated to Kunde; Girmi may have been born in Tibet as well. There were four other children; only Urken is still alive. As a youngster she did a lot of portering for expeditions, but she couldn't recall which ones (the high-altitude sherpa jobs have almost always gone to men). As a married woman she had four children, none of which lived to adulthood. She and her husband adopted the son of a relative:

> So finally her husband's relative had a son, they had several children, and had hard time to feed them, so they just, you know, took the first son from the family and kept feeding him and feeding him and he just became, as their son, which is now Lhakpa Tsering, and Lhakpa Tsering has climbed Mt. Everest, too.

From the registry of the Himalayan Club I knew that Girmi had been on a number of expeditions before ours: Everest in 1953,

Kangchenjunga in 1955, Everest again in 1956 and 1960, and Makalu in 1961. He was also with the Hillary scientific expedition of 1960-61, as was Barry Bishop, one of the summit climbers in 1963. Bishop and Girmi bonded on the earlier trip, and their bonding was evident in 1963; Girmi was Bishop's personal sherpa, and a devoted one, comparable to Ang Dawa and our leader Norman Dyhrenfurth. I think both members felt as close to their sherpas as they might have to brothers, and it looked mutual.

Urken Doma, sister of Girmi Dorje, Kunde

Urken said that after 1963 Girmi lived mainly in Kathmandu, working the occasional expedition and possibly doing some guiding for trekkers. He was with three Japanese expeditions, the second of which was the infamous 1970 "ski expedition", organized by a mystical Japanese who had made it his life-or-death ambition to ski down Everest. Seven Sherpas died in one accident in the icefall, and at that point Girmi's wife (or possibly his sister) rushed to Base

Camp and spent seven days there trying to persuade him to give it up. As we've seen, most Sherpas who experience this demand acquiesce; Girmi would not. He survived, and went on to join another Japanese expedition (his third with them), this time to Gangapurna in 1973. It was his last.

———

Sherap had found out that a helicopter was bringing a few guests to the Everest View on the next day and suggested that I could take the helicopter out from the Syangboche airstrip. The idea of skipping the two-day hike back to Lukla had a great appeal, greater than I liked admitting, so we hiked back up to the airstrip, in perfect weather, and I spent the late afternoon and night there, thinking about my next moves and re-organizing my notes (something I had to do every day).

> 2/24: Up at least 3 times in the night. At 6:30 the scene looks completely fogged in! By 7 some clearing, a little blue sky. But rapid change, mostly for worse. 7:45 socked in again. Prospect: wait it out, or set off with Sherap for Namche and then on towards Lukla (9-10 hours more of hiking). Grim! Right now can hardly think about it. I sit by the fire in the kitchen, with the servant blowing on it, child chattering next to me, something unappetizing bubbling in a big pot. Lhasa Apso pushing for attention. What time will Sherap arrive? (I'm hoping for better weather too much!) On the shelves, Chivas Regal, Snickers and Mars bars, Fanta.

I suppose the morning dawned but there was no sign of it. The sky had dropped to ankle-level, the airstrip and the yaks dotted around it were all covered with snow, and clearly unless something remarkable happened to the weather there would be no helicopter. I waited until 10:30 for word from Kathmandu (by telephone), but wasn't surprised to hear the flight had definitely been canceled. While waiting I tried to warm myself by a wood stove, and watched a flickering TV picture with nothing but static for sound. It turned out to be a form of self-torture, because the only channel available featured a documentary on body-piercing in Southern California with many scenes shot at the sun-drenched beach and along the palm-tree-lined palisades of Santa Monica, where I had spent several days just a few weeks before.

Traffic on the trek

The only thing for it was to drag the old bones back down to Namche, and then further down to Lukla. It was misting for most of the trip and threatening to rain, and slippery underfoot. Trudging along in the wet, gray air I had vivid flashbacks of the return march to Kathmandu 35 years ago. It was June then and the monsoons had begun, bringing unending rain in quantities I had never imagined.

> 2/26: Hoping for heat in the dining room but found only 3 sticks of incense burning. Weather completely clear, everything looking much more hospitable then yesterday in the rain. Some mud had turned back to dust. Girl putting up her long black hair outside her doorway. Beautiful child wandering meditatively down the street. (Even the chickens looked beautiful)

DARJEELING

Unless you have done it often, it's disorienting to beam down from Khumbu to Kathmandu in 35 minutes. The contrast is extreme on almost any dimension you can think of: altitude, population density, ethnic variety, vehicular traffic, air quality, commercial activity, noise, or sense of what century you are in. I grew to like Kathmandu, even with its truly frightening pollution, but still it was a shock. Images of Khumbu stayed in my head.

> 2/27: Of course with all these contacts and interactions, I'm into my comfort zone again, and feel at home and like life makes sense again. Contrast with loneliness and vulnerability I felt in Khumbu, where I was trying (I think) to play out some quasi-heroic role -- doing it alone, taking it as it came, no softening of edges, etc. (Meet any challenge.) Where the hell did that come from?

I was back in Kathmandu just long enough to make arrangements for the trip to Darjeeling. A Sherpa friend recommended the overnight bus ride to India, but I didn't relish 12 hours in a crowded bus with probably little sleep; call me a coward, but the low cost didn't seem to offset the lengthy discomfort. Instead, Stan Armington of Malla Trek got me on the flight to Biratnagar in the easternmost part of Nepal, and arranged for a taxi to meet me there for the trip to the border. There I would have to switch to an Indian taxi for a ride to the town of Siliguri, and there choose how I wanted to cover the final leg up into the hills to Darjeeling.

Darjeeling was on the itinerary for several reasons. Many Sherpas migrated there in the first half of the century, and the now-famous Sherpa reputation was first established there. Further, the town is famous as perhaps the most beautiful example of the colonial British hill-towns, places to which colonists and other expatriates retreated from the heat of summer in the Indian plains. What may be its most famous attraction is the view it offers of the eastern end of the Himalayas, and, literally above all, the massif of Kangchenjunga, only 30 miles or so distant as the crow flies. But I would have gone even without these reasons, in order to meet with two Sherpas who had migrated there a long time ago and stayed, separating themselves from the traditional life in Khumbu. They were Nawang Gombu, the summiteer of 1963 and the "frolicking Gombu" of my Sherpa tour of the U.S., and Ang Dawa, Dyhrenfurth's personal sherpa and long-time friend (and another member of the tour).

Biratnagar is Nepal's second-largest city. In March it is a flat, hot, and dusty town at sea level with nothing other than its airport to recommend it to tourists (in fact, Stan had warned me, "Whatever happens, don't stay overnight in Biratnagar!"). It is a terminus for tourists going into or coming out of the Terai, the tropical region of Nepal lying along the southern border with India, or for tourists like me wanting to get to Darjeeling and Sikkim to the east. I saw almost nothing of it; the taxi was waiting and we sped off as soon as the driver and I had found one another.

He, and the friend he had brought along, spoke almost no English so conversation was out. This left me concentrating on how long my life might last in the hands of this driver, or probably of any other from Biratnagar. The two-lane road going east had a decent surface at first but was in use by all kinds of voyagers: pedestrians, cyclists, rickshaws, cargo platforms on wheels pulled by cattle, motorcycles, autos, and small and large trucks. The game was to pass as many of these obstacles as possible in the shortest time. Almost all the cars and trucks I saw maintained a position as near the middle of the road as they could get, at least two wheels over the center-line, until they might be forced back into their own lane by something as large as a car or truck coming toward them; nothing smaller was threatening enough. Being ready to pass, even if nothing was in sight, was paramount. A heavy hand on the horn had long ago become an unconscious habit. Of course it was useful, even necessary, for maneuvering through the stream of traffic on the road, but it almost never stopped—my driver once even beeped at a speed-bump in the road. The hour-long flight on the plane had been a slight nightmare caused by the screaming, I should say the most piercing, angry and alarming screaming I've ever heard, of a baby whom no one could quiet; the mother, the grandmother, the flight attendant, and random passengers all tried with no success. Only the pilot never had a shot at it. The baby had staying power and should do well in life, but after an hour I was desperate to get off the plane. Alas, after only a few minutes of relative silence, my taxi's horn filled the void for most of the four-hour ride to the border.

We traveled on a wide, flat plain, nearly at sea level. The mountains that dominate most people's image of Nepal were out of sight, replaced by fields and bullocks and huts as far as one could see. The road-side villages were of bamboo and wattle, often on stilts, with fronds for roofs, and they teemed with people. For more than half the distance the road was under construction which meant it was rough, we were often off on an even rougher detour into dirt, and traffic got compressed into a tightly packed chain of smoke-spewing trucks and cars. The road work was usually a gaggle of young women with a sprinkling of old ones, all on their haunches with a broom or board smoothing gravel, or just sweeping the dirt surface. Men were doing the "technical" work, like changing the STOP-GO sign, or measuring the roadbed with a tape-measure. No signs in English here, except for the bridges, which curiously each had an English name, and beer ads (mainly Tuborg and Tiger). In complete opposition to the bird world, men were invariably in drab clothes while the women were everywhere in brilliant saturated hues, especially red, green, blue, and purple. This kind of setting, so mundane for them but so exotic for a boy from St. Louis, Missouri, always sends me into a state of heightened sensibility; a brief sighting of a distant woman in red sitting on a rock in the middle of a dry and tan riverbed could make me feel I understood, at last, Romantic painting.

At the border, I emerged from the car and was immediately surrounded by shouting and gesturing Indians who wanted my business for the next leg. I settled on one, and armed with an idea of what the price ought to be, I was negotiating with the driver, who naturally wanted more. The throng of competing drivers was all around us, listening closely, and one leaned in the window to accept the price I was offering. This nearly led to a fight, but it was useful as a bargaining chip and I got close to the target price. Unfortunately, no sooner had I gone through the border formalities, first in the Nepalese hut and then the Indian, than my driver discovered a completely flattened tire, and passed me on to another driver. He had my thanks, though, because he passed along the agreed-on price and there was no new round of haggling.

Two more hours got us to the larger but no less flat, hot and dusty town of Siliguri. My plan had been to stay there overnight and take the famous narrow-gauge railway up to Darjeeling, but we were in Siliguri by 4 p.m., the sun was still high, and it seemed too early to stop. So I went into the center of town and a spot where jeeps for Darjeeling and Sikkim wait for a full load of passengers before taking off. Doing it this way, without a schedule, keeps the cost very low and is how the locals all do it. The downside, I found, was that the sun was not nearly so high when we finally got on the road, we made many stops letting people and cargo on and off before we ever actually got going, and then we were packed in four across with no windows to hold off the wind which got colder and colder as the sun went down and we got higher and higher.

In Darjeeling I chose to stay in an old but reputedly elegant hotel recommended by a friend who had stayed there 20 years ago. After arriving in the dark, dealing with the crowd of porters who wanted to carry my bag to the hotel, and finally checking into the place, I was delighted to be alone again and in a quiet room. Plenty of solitude here! After dinner in a spooky dining room, lit only by candles on the tables, in which I was the sole diner, served by two waiters wearing white gloves and turbans, and entertained by an older, middle-European looking woman with an incurable cough (caused by Darjeeling smoke as I later found out) playing a marginal piano, I slept soundly and dreamt metaphorically of Kangchenjunga.

> 3/1: At around 8 went for dinner -- room lit only by 26 candles, + pianist! Lots of good tasting food, esp onions with apple au gratin, mushroom potatoes, ham, carrots, great torte with brown sugar, and special Indian coffee. // The merely 3 hour drive had seemed endless, but I was less panicky about what I'm doing. Now in room with coal fire and electric heater. I'll call Gombu tomorrow and get to work! (I have to note a fear in the background that maybe my body will somehow break down -- back, stomach, other illness -- like some of the ancient cars I've been riding in.)

> Random note: Once you've had traveller's diarrhea on a trip you have only to ask the question, how does my stomach feel? to start something happening...

The morning revealed a Darjeeling that was sitting literally in the clouds. Visibility was 100 yards at best, through a kind of brown fog created by the smoke from many coal fires blending with the prevailing mist. This hardly changed during the several days I was there and my closest acquaintance with the vaunted views from Darjeeling is still the 1926 Cook's brochure. (Earl Denman had arrived there at almost exactly the same time 51 years earlier with an Everest glint in his eye, but I had forgotten what he wrote: "There was a thick, damp mist through which little could be seen...The weather was cold and dismal, permitting no view of the mountains...") The chances for the success of my trip now lay entirely with my Sherpas.

And they delivered. Gombu had returned early from a trip to Calcutta which I didn't know he was making. And Ang Dawa had his son drive him for the five-hour trip from Gangtok, Sikkim. I didn't feel worthy of these sacrifices, but I was none the less grateful for that. I was able to spend much of the first day with them, and I saw immediately that nothing had changed between these two. On our tour of the U.S. in 1963 Ang Dawa had slyly referred to Gombu as a "Big Man," and himself as merely a "Little Man," referring to Gombu's tendency to take over any social situation, put himself in the spotlight, speak for others, and the like. In theory, when I was interviewing Ang Dawa, Gombu was supposed to be merely translating. But in fact he often simply answered my question to Ang Dawa himself, as if he knew what Ang Dawa would say or felt he could give a better answer. He also frequently turned Ang Dawa's answers toward some topic with Gombu at the center. It sounds exasperating and in a way it was. But Gombu has such boyish charm and enthusiasm that you can't stay exasperated for long.

―――――

Nawang Gombu was born in or about 1936 in Khumjung. His mother was Tenzing Norgay's sister, his father a Tibetan trader and a religious man who would have preferred being a monk.

Nawang Gombu, Ang Dawa, and Ang Dawa's youngest son, Darjeeling

Failing that, he hoped to see Gombu become a monk. On his second trading trip into Tibet with his father, at somewhere between ten and twelve years old, Gombu was left at the Rongbuk monastery with the understanding that he would stay there for five years, as indeed his father had done as a boy.

This was to be the start of a Buddhist education and his establishment as a monk. Such an education was all that was available in Khumbu at that time and was generally considered to be a privilege, but for Gombu it was something else entirely. The monastery sits at about 17,000 feet, nearly a mile higher than Khumjung, and the monastic life especially for students was not designed for comfort. The worst thing, however, and the most surprising to me in the light of my (admittedly superficial) understanding of Buddhism, was that punishment seemed to be the main pedagogic technique.

> It was cold weather, it's almost 17,000 feet, the Rongbuk, you know, and then we don't have really firewood, only yak dung, you have to burn the fire and then cook your food, like that. And must be about 300 students, and ...I'm the youngest one in the school, you know. But is, I mean, the punishment is such a way, that if you mistake about 100 words, that means you got bamboo stick, you know, little bit, you have to blow up your cheek, you know, like that [demonstrates], and they give you about 200 [blows] here [points to cheek]. And it happened here, and then you have to do another one, here, you know [points to other cheek]. And then, other one, hard part, is if you mistake more than 200 then you have to open your pants and you get, like leather belt, you know, and they give your bottom, you know—it's—teacher is so hard there, punishment is real hard. I mean, you can't sit in the daytime, you know. And sometimes, I remember very well, I can't open my mouth. eating the food, you know. Then I tell Ang Tsering, let's, I want to escape.

Another escape! But this time Gombu wanted to get back to

Khumbu rather than to leave it; he had been thrown into a situation to which the life of a trader compared very favorably, he thought.

The Ang Tsering he mentions is the same Ang Tsering in whose house in Khumjung I had stayed just before coming to Darjeeling.

> He say, How you escape? I say, in the moonlight. And we got tsampa, we got butter...And then one day we went bathroom, and we see the place. And I say Ok, now...I say, Ang Tsering, look, we go to the bathroom and from there we jump outside, and then we go. This is how Ang Tsering and I did, you know. It was midnight, it was almost 12 o'clock, and we jumped from there, and then all night we are walking, right down from the road and finally we reached...a yak hut. And then we stopped there, and the yak man told me, What happened? And I said, we went to school, now we're going back home. They gave us the cheese and food, everything.

Gombu was hazy about dates but this would have been about 1949 as far as I can tell. He had been over the Nangpa La twice on trading trips so he was familiar with the territory, but it's still slightly breathtaking to think of two early adolescents wandering through such mountains with little food or clothing (they made boots by stuffing grass in whatever they were wearing as foot-cover). It looks again as if the boys counted on the kindness of strangers and were not disappointed. His father was angry, of course, and gave him "a couple of slaps." But his mother said, more compassionately, "If he doesn't like it why are you making him do it?" and that seems to have been the end of it. Gombu was back in the routine of trading trips to Tibet.

With Tenzing for an uncle Gombu was exposed to talk about mountaineering from an early age and as with many of the other enterprising Sherpas it began to work on him. But he was saved the trouble of running to Darjeeling for work. In 1952 Tenzing came through Namche Bazar with a Swiss expedition, the first to attempt the ascent of Everest from the Nepalese side. It was the first time

Gombu's uncle had been back to Khumbu in 18 years, and his friends and relatives (including Gombu) made it a memorable occasion. Tenzing remembered:

> When at last we reached Namche there was a great reunion, not only for myself, but for all the Sherpas who had been long away... The news of our coming had, of course, gone before us, and it seemed that every Sherpa in the world was there, ready to welcome us and celebrate ...They brought gifts. They brought food and chang. And so did almost all the people of Khumbu ...and we all joined together in singing, dancing, and drinking...

It was a turning point for Gombu. Although he hadn't been hired as a porter he went to Base Camp with the expedition, and managed to talk Tenzing into taking him back to Darjeeling with him when it was over. That put him in a privileged position for being hired as a sherpa for the British effort in 1953, at the age of 17. Wilfrid Noyce described his early impression of him:

> Gompu [sic] was one of the most intriguing of the characters. On the march, being rather fat, he had been the only Sherpa ever to have been heard to ask a sahib if he would walk slower. Yet he was one of the two to reach the top of Kang Cho, though only seventeen; and he later carried his load to the South Col. The son of a lama...he took life very seriously. He was also one of the two Sherpas able to write. (Noyce, p. 95)

Gombu's face seems particularly to have stuck with Noyce; his narrative is sprinkled with such references as, "...with the homely face of Gompu once more appearing behind the soup," and "...behind which the round, grinning face of Gompu..."

Besides capturing the members' attention with his looks and personality, Gombu performed very well. He carried loads twice to the South Col and was there to meet Tenzing and Hillary when they returned from the summit and to accompany them back to Base Camp. He must by that time have felt a strong connection to the mountain. Noyce gave his later impression of Gombu on the return march to Kathmandu, after the action was all over:

> Gompu himself, like Mr. Pickwick, had grown in stature from a round and laughable character as you came to know him. He had over other Sherpas the great advantage of being able to read and write. This gave him, as he scuttled up and down on the self-appointed task of checking coolies, the air of an earnest sergeant.

After the expedition he returned to Darjeeling, where he has lived ever since. In 1954 Tenzing and the Chief Minister for West Bengal planned and set up an Indian mountaineering school, to be called the Himalayan Mountaineering Institute (HMI). Tenzing was to be in charge of instruction. They contacted the Swiss Foundation for Alpine Research which sent out to them the head of a Swiss climbing school to help with organizing the Indian one. Among the first six instructors Tenzing hired were Ang Tharkay and Tenzing's two nephews, Topgay and Gombu. When Tenzing retired from the position of Field Director in 1976, Gombu succeeded him and has continued in the post up to the day of our interview at the Windamere Hotel.

In 1954, after several months of mountaineering training in Switzerland, Gombu was on his second expedition, this time to Makalu (27,824 feet) in the Everest vicinity with the California Himalayan Expedition led by Will Siri, who in 1963 would be Deputy Leader of AMEE. (Willi Unsoeld was another member of the Makalu team.) In 1957 he climbed to within a few hundred feet of the summit of Nanda Devi (25,645 feet), a devilishly difficult mountain, with an Indian expedition but was turned back by the weather. Along the way:

> ...Gombu and his rope-mates were suddenly caught in a small avalanche. By instinct, Gombu had thrown his arms and legs about and had managed to keep his head above to save himself but it had been an experience that Gombu is unlikely to forget. (Sastry, p. 20)

That is exactly how I remembered Gombu from our U.S. trip in 1963: throwing his arms and legs about—in the swimming pool, on the trampoline, in the bowling alley, on the driving range, he held nothing back.

In 1959 Gombu was selected to accompany the International Women's Expedition to Cho Oyu (26,760 feet), whose members included Gombu's sister Doma and Tenzing's two daughters. That expedition ended abruptly when four Sherpas and two members were killed in an avalanche. In 1960 he returned to Everest, again with an Indian expedition, and this time in spite of bad weather he and two others reached 28,300 feet before turning back.

This crescendo of climbing climaxed with Gombu's selection for AMEE. Because of his status at the HMI, his experience, and perhaps because of his facility with language, he was treated as a member rather than as a sherpa, and his strong performance fully validated that "promotion." There were political overtones to his member status, however, and especially to his selection as a summit candidate. Gombu and Ang Dawa were two of only four Sherpas from Darjeeling; all the others were from Khumbu, and the Khumbu Sherpas had some proprietary feelings about their Nepalese mountains. In fact, Gombu told me he felt he was selected because of recommendations by Siri and Unsoeld, not by Jimmy Roberts. Roberts, he felt, "favored" Khumbu Sherpas. There was probably resentment but it never amounted to a crisis.

Two weeks before Gombu's summit day Lute Jerstad noted in his diary: "Gombu is very happy now that the big day draws near. He said he has never seen climbing to match our performance. He is practically one of us now and is delighted to be part of the first assault team." (Jerstad, p. 91)

RETURN TO THE SCENE OF THE CLIMB

Lute's diary entry about the return of Whittaker and Gombu from the summit to the South Col is one of those passages that makes people wonder why mountaineers do it:

> The physical nightmare they had been through was written on their faces. Jim resembled an old man, 30 years older. His face was heavily lined, his eyes were bloodshot, and his skin was blue. I've never seen a man age so much in so few hours in all my life. Gombu didn't look much better. (Jerstad, p. 120)

The experience certainly did not deter Gombu. In 1964 he climbed to the summit of Nanda Devi, and in 1965 he went once again to the peak of the Everest pyramid. He was much honored as the first person to climb Everest twice.

Gombu went on his last Himalayan expedition in 1982. Jim Whittaker's twin brother, Lou, was organizing a joint Chinese-American Everest expedition via Tibet, following the old British route, and invited Gombu to come along. Gombu was now approaching 50, still fit but not a prime candidate for a climbing member. However, Gombu had a very personal reason for wanting to go, and it had nothing to do with his connection with Everest or his friendship with the Whittakers. It had to do with that painful year spent at the Rongbuk monastery:

> I want to see the monastery, you know, that's why I went. That's why I joined with him, you know. And, monastery is completely destroyed! All gone. And then we came back, and the people say, Gombu, you want to try third time the Everest? I said, No. They say, why you came here? I said, I studied Rongbuk monastery when I was very young, that's why I wanted to see the monastery.

The Chinese had destroyed Rongbuk along with many other Buddhist monasteries, as part of their imposition of Communist Chinese culture on Tibet. Somehow, Gombu hadn't heard about it.

After the Chinese-American expedition the Chinese threw a big banquet, at which the president of the Chinese Mountaineering Association told Gombu that it was not the Chinese but the Tibetans who destroyed the monastery (almost unthinkable in light of the role of the monasteries in Tibetan life). Rather than argue, Gombu simply replied in the strongest terms that the Chinese had a responsibility to restore the monastery, and in fact it appears that they now have done so. Gombu has still not seen it, but may yet go back. He seems to be reminiscing a lot about his early days in Khumbu.

Gombu has three daughters and a son. One daughter, Rita, is one of the few women to have climbed on Everest. [Many hundreds of women have summitted since that time.] She made it to within 300 feet of the summit; apparently she could have gone on but stopped to help another Sherpani with frostbitten feet. She now works for the Air India Tourism Department. A second daughter, Yangdu, has her own travel agency in New Delhi, arranging trekking and river-rafting outings over the whole Ladakh-Nepal-Sikkim region. The third daughter, Ong Mo, has finished college and works in the export division of the Duracell Company. Gombu's son is now in Toronto, Canada.

> 3/2: Gombu crashed his car recently, now in Siliguri for repairs (3 months). He laughs, "I was lucky," but feels all in car could have been killed (wife, several others). Collided with a truck, says it was his fault.

As Gombu and I were finishing our interview on the veranda of the Windamere and I was savoring the pitiful glimmerings of sunlight that made it through the soupy air, tiny Ang Dawa showed up. He had with him his youngest son, who had driven him up to Darjeeling from Gangtok. None of the three wanted to share my formal, white-gloved midday meal, and I was paying too much to consider skipping it, so we agreed to meet again in the afternoon.

Ang Dawa is small even for a Sherpa. He is proof of the old saw about not judging books by their covers, because time and time again he has proven himself stronger than men with much more imposing physiques. Everything about him projects humility, along with a sunniness and sense of humor that makes Dyhrenfurth's repeated choice of him as his personal sherpa easy to understand (Norman once wrote to me, "I loved him like my brother"). Of course one needs more than cheerfulness in a sherpa; Ang Dawa's endurance, steadfastness and loyalty are less visible in a social encounter but nonetheless part of his character.

Our interview started on a note of ambiguity and never got far past it. There are a number of Ang Dawas mentioned in the mountaineering literature and I'm not sure which ones are this one. The interview should have settled it, but between Ang Dawa's very halting English (although he is fluent in several other languages) and his evident unease with being in the spotlight, and Gombu's assertive interpretations and invasive interpolations, a lot of information I think was lost to me. We finally deduced that Ang Dawa was probably born between 1925 and 1928, although both he and his son started out by giving his birthdate as 1937. He was born in Namche Bazar, and his early memories not surprisingly are of trips to Tibet across the Nangpa La. He had two brothers but both of these died of exposure coming over the Nangpa La in a blizzard, on a trading trip.

Sometime in the late 1940s, in his late teens or early twenties, Ang Dawa ran away from Namche to Darjeeling with a friend. Any details he might have given me about how he pulled this off were buried by Gombu in an avalanche of generalizations instead of translations: "This is what usually we do. Because this is how I went 1952 expedition, you know. There's a lot of Sherpas come like that." Exasperating! The only fact about Ang Dawa's life in Darjeeling that I could find, like an arm sticking out of the snow when the avalanche settled, was that Tenzing Norgay picked out the girl he should marry and Ang Dawa followed his advice. This was one of the few marriages I heard about that hadn't been arranged by parents; Ang Dawa apparently pursued the girl on his own, won her, and fathered three sons with her.

Ang Dawa already had an impressive list of climbing experiences in his background when he was recruited for AMEE. Norman has verified that our Ang Dawa was with Maurice Herzog when he climbed Annapurna in 1950 (the first successful climb of a major Himalayan peak), with the Swiss expedition to Everest in 1952, with Norman on Lhotse in 1955, on an expedition searching for the Yeti in 1958, with Norman again in 1960 on Dhaulagiri, and then on Everest in 1963, when he was (probably) in his 40s, and when he accompanied Norman to over 28,000 feet.

With such experience Ang Dawa was second only to Gombu in the hierarchy of Sherpas, and the two of them (plus Bishop's sherpa Girmi Dorje) were throughout considered candidates for a summit team. Indeed if Norman had been able to keep going as he tried to film Whittaker and Gombu ahead of him, or if he had been selfishly willing to abandon Norman for a couple of hours, Ang Dawa would certainly have become the third Sherpa to have made it there.

I've already mentioned how, several days before the planned summit effort, Norman's oxygen regulator began to malfunction. Here is some more detail:

> The regulator on Norman's apparatus sprang a leak. Instead of going to his lungs, part of the gas passing from cylinder to mask seeped out into the air with a depressing hiss, and there were neither effective tools at hand to fix it nor spare regulators for replacement. Ang Dawa, whose devotion to his Bara Sah'b was total, immediately insisted on exchanging regulators. But Norman said no; Ang Dawa, no less than he, would soon be going all out to reach Everest's summit and must also have a dependable oxygen flow. (Ullman, p. 179)

Gombu went to the other Sherpas in the camp but none would give up his regulator; probably a reflection of the Darjeeling-Khumbu tensions, Norman felt. In any case, "Ang Dawa spent the night and the next day with the leaking oxygen gear." One of the Sherpas eventually did trade equipment with Ang Dawa, but on the first night on the South Col another problem developed: there were 12 men in the camp but only 11 sleeping bags. Worse, when this was discovered, eight of the bags were already in the possession of the eight rank-and-file Sherpas, and another confrontation between Khumbu and Darjeeling threatened. Again, it was Ang Dawa to the rescue: "Once more it was Ang Dawa who, at his own insistence, made the sacrifice: sleeping without a bag and, swathed in double layers of clothing, wedging himself as tightly as possible between Big Jim and Gombu." (Ullman, p. 173)

Nor was the oxygen problem solved finally. On the day of the establishment of the highest camp on Everest (27,450 feet) Ang Dawa had ended up with the faulty regulator again and Norman's best efforts were unable to fix it. It was only when they had reached the high camp that Dawa Tenzing, who had carried a load to that point, gave up his own regulator to Ang Dawa.

Norman and Ang Dawa followed on behind Whittaker and Gombu, carrying loads of photographic equipment of around 50 pounds each and hoping to reach the South Summit from which Norman could film the actual reaching of the summit. But at a little over 28,000 feet Norman's good sense overcame the dream of a lifetime:

> The little Sherpa wanted to go on. 'But I explained to him...that this was the point of no return. If we went on, we would run out of oxygen about halfway between the South Summit and the Main Summit, and that would be that: we would never get down alive [both Norman and Ang Dawa were in their middle 40s]. Also, we couldn't reach the Main Summit, so we wouldn't even be dead heroes on the top of Everest.' (Ullman, p. 184)

I'm not sure that Ang Dawa understood this explanation. His reply apparently was to point toward the summit and say, "Up go, Bara Sah'b?" Only five feet tall, but as Ullman wrote, "every inch indomitable."

Ang Dawa was still on the job two days later, as the summit and support teams were descending below the South Col:

> ...their legs were rubbery, their energy low, their reactions sluggish, and time and time again there were slips on the loose snow and rotten rock. Once Barry peeled off altogether and began falling, but was held on the rope by Ang Dawa. (Ullman, p. 204-5)

And when Tom Hornbein saw Norman and his sherpa making their painful way back to Base Camp he noted, "Ang Dawa still moved like a lithe spider monkey..."

Somewhere in the early 1960s, Ang Dawa began working as an instructor for the Indian government at their climbing school in Sikkim. Their many student field trips into the high Himalaya were often or usually into areas close to the Chinese border and combined training with information-gathering. This is not to say that Ang Dawa was an intelligence agent, and in fact he may not have known what intelligence was being gathered when he took groups into the mountains. If he did, I certainly couldn't get him to tell me about it, even in his retirement.

However, he didn't mind talking about a curious episode that turned out to involve members of AMEE. I had heard rumors of this episode for years but only in 1998 did I get hold of a few facts. In 1965 and again in 1966 a covert "special project" was mounted jointly by the Indian and United States governments to find out whether or not China had the capability to launch an ICBM. It was suspected that they were carrying out tests in Tibet, and the idea was to set up an electronic sensor on a high Himalayan peak for continuous monitoring of the alleged testing. (I assume that later this kind of intelligence would be gathered by satellite but in the mid-'60s such satellites had not yet been positioned in space.) The sensor required power, of course, and once set up was to run by itself for long periods of time. The power requirement was to be provided by a small nuclear generator. That's what caused the trouble.

In 1965 Ang Dawa as well as at least two members of AMEE were participants in the team that carried the generator-sensor system high on Nanda Devi (25,645 feet). The sensor may have been set on top—that wasn't made clear in the interview—but the generator was installed somewhere below the summit. The "trouble" was that several months later, when the team went to check on it, they were unable to find it! Had it simply been covered by heavy snowfall? Or had it fallen from its perch, possibly all the way to the river at the base of the mountain, where it might be unceasingly polluting part of India's water supply? The "loss" of a nuclear generator was serious business. Somehow news of all this got into the Indian press and made front-page stories for a while. The possibility that CIA incompetence was responsible for threats to Indian lives got heavy play. So far as I know the generator has never been found.

Unfortunately for Gombu, he had climbed Nanda Devi in 1964. Although he was with a merely conventional climbing expedition and it was a year earlier, when the Indian papers noticed the coincidence they made much of it. Was an Indian hero mixed up with the CIA? What did he know and when did he know it? Gombu had to spend a lot of time on the telephone and on radio shows protesting his innocence, and his visibility in India became much higher as a result of it. (None of this affected Ang Dawa who, as a Little Man, was unknown to the press.)

Apparently a second team returned to Nanda Devi in 1966 to look further for the generator, and this time a third ex-member of AMEE was in charge of the operation. Six months were allotted for the search, but half-way through, the leader had become so frustrated by Indian bureaucracy that he simply left.

Ang Dawa had a long career with the Sikkim climbing school, and has now retired with a government pension. Of his three sons, one works "for the press" in Sikkim, another works for an insurance company in Siliguri, and the third is just now unemployed.

———

Ang Dawa and his son left for Gantok, and I spent another day with Gombu: touring the HMI; standing on the hill above HMI where Tenzing Norgay is buried and honored with a statue, thinking about the history of climbing on Everest since Tenzing and Hillary paved the way for today's unimagined commercialization; and sharing food and drink in Gombu's fine house.

> 3/3: Visited Tenzing's grave site. Then down to Gombu's house for tea and cookies, then beer and chips, and he was bringing out Momos when I decided I had to leave (tummy not up to this). Felt weak, Gombu sent Sherpa with me to HMI gate, he insisted on carrying my camera case! Walked around further on my own, but very slowly. Nothing looks attractive or interesting to me, just daily life and lots of signs of decay.

In the evening, one last Windamere dinner, at which I thought if I have to listen one more time to this pianist's rendition of "Stardust" I will go mad, and then early to bed in order to get an early morning start on the drive back to Biratnagar.

KATHMANDU

> 3/4: JIM: Pull back from negative thoughts -- DON'T leave here early and leave something useful undone! Identify priorities, then fit the time to that. GOT THAT?

Once more back in Kathmandu, ensconced in a $10 room at the Kathmandu Guest House, I made the many phone calls it took to find and arrange meetings with my last Sherpa interviewees. The most interesting looked to be Nima Tenzing, the last of the three surviving members of my Sherpa tour of the United States, and Kalden, who after a trekking career had now gone back to being a monk.

Nima Tenzing today is the proprietor of Nepal Tenzing Adventure Trekking (P) Ltd. His large house and lodge ("Sherpa House") is in a quiet residential section of Kathmandu, hard to find in a maze of small streets if you don't know the way. I managed it by going to the nearby Shangri-La Hotel on a main road, where an employee of Nima's met me and walked me to the house. Because Nima on the phone seemed to be fairly fluent in English I decided to interview him without an interpreter; I feared bringing one along would be an insult. Indeed, he has a surprising vocabulary. But his pronunciation often made his sentences opaque to me and more than once I wished for Sherap.

Nima, like many of the others of the class of '63, has come a long way. Besides gaining a lot of weight he's gained an aura of authority. My base line, of course, was the tour in 1963, when he seemed deferential and a bit shy—not at all surprising for a Sherpa on his first trip to a strange culture. Today he's socially skilled and outspoken, free with criticism even of other Sherpas, and has obviously been in charge in a lot of situations.

Nima Tenzing, Kathmandu

He was born about 1939 in the village of Thame, Tenzing Norgay's birthplace, in Khumbu. His father, like most fathers in Khumbu, was a farmer who kept some yaks as well; Nima's childhood was largely a matter of yak-watching (you may remember that a yak injured one of his eyes) and helping with the farm jobs. He stuck it out until he was 12 or 13 and then ran away —to Darjeeling of course. Ang Dawa, I learned on this trip, is Nima's uncle, and he was already there. One might get the impression that Khumbu villages generally lost all their males over 14 to middle-of-the-night migrations to Darjeeling. Obviously this didn't happen. It's just that when you focus on Sherpas of this era who involved themselves in expedition work you are surely looking at an unusually ambitious group, who had to take a lot of initiative in order to get involved. And further, Sherpas born in Nima's era who wanted to connect with the world of expeditions had to go to Darjeeling; it simply could not be done in Nepal at that time.

> I escaped in the middle night. Parents sleeping, so I escaped (laughter from unidentified relative across the room). We make a plan. So in nighttime, you know, we have big doors, same as this kind, and they harder to open, you know, too noisy (simulates). So I try many times, it doesn't work. Later I use my imagination. I went into kitchen, one cup water and put in the drawer. And the wood get wet, after, no noise, so I can escape, you know (laughter).

Nima and a friend hiked as far as Siliguri, and from there took the train into the hills. This would have been in the early 1950s. He seemed to say that Tenzing was teaching other Sherpas in Darjeeling the basics of rock-climbing and expedition work, and that Tenzing hired him as a sherpa on some of the trekking and minor climbing expeditions for which he was sirdar. Nima says he was a fast learner and naturally good at mountaineering, so that he was busy and out in the field most of the time. But he was strongly ambitious and keen to learn everything he could.

> I was daytime working hotel, nighttime I go the pastry shop, how to bake the bread, biscuit, scones, all the stuff. But they pay nothing for me, maybe one rupee a night, but I was not interested rupees, I was to learn. I did it. So after I finish everything I took the double job. I was guide, and cook. I made the double salary.

I understood that he came back to Nepal, along with many other Sherpas from Darjeeling, sometime later in the 1950s, after the government had begun allowing foreigners to travel within the country. He worked in the field for the Swiss geologist Toni Hagen, who has given the most complete account of the formation of the Himalayan range.

...and the guy who came the first who writed the books, you know, Toni Hagen, I was working with him. We were six guys with him, for almost three-four years. We have trouble every village. At that time nobody knows how many nationalities Nepal had. We're now 14 different nationalities.

Nima spoke off-handedly of going on many expeditions before AMEE, including probably all of the ones of which Dyhrenfurth had been either member or leader, and also including four Yeti-searching efforts.

Nima was on at least two more mountaineering expeditions after AMEE, both Japanese. In 1964 he was a climbing sherpa on an expedition that sounded disastrous as he described it. The Japanese involved had little or no expedition experience, as became obvious very early:

> Almost a non-organized expedition. They forget all the things, the packages from the company in Japan. (JL: They forgot them?) They did not send the equipment. They only sent the sake, sakes and wines and beers (laughter). So we reached Base Camp, it's terrible, it's snowing, you know, afternoon. So we opened the boxes, get the equipment. No equipment! ... gloves, sleeping bags, there was none. One Japanese guy they call the equipment master, he say, We are Japan, never make mistakes. It was packed, everything's here, you know. I told him, everybody can make mistake. He must check. So we opened all boxes, couldn't found it. What to do? Set up the tent, but no clothes. So I went to Namche, we rented, I went to my home, bought the rucksacks, ..., woolens, socks, everything. And I brought 16 sleeping bags from my home, and we rented Namche about 16.

Nima's experiences on the trip went seriously downhill from there. As a kind of climax, he was sherpa for the two-man summit team, and he explained the night before their summit effort that they must get an early start to avoid the danger of avalanches. They agreed to start by 6:30 a.m., but by 10:30 they had still not come out of their tents. They managed to get going by 11, but very soon after insisted on stopping for lunch. Still they were determined, if that's the right word, to try for the summit. Some time later they were all wrapped in a white-out, so surrounded by fog and snow that nothing at all could be seen. The three were roped together, and Nima tied his end of the rope to a rock to stabilize their situation. But when he tried to move to the other two he found they were gone. They had apparently unhooked from the rope and had fallen at least 25 feet to a ledge and were unable to climb back up.

According to Nima's story, he radioed to the next camp below them for help; the reply came back that someone would set out. But by 8:30 in the evening no one had yet come. Nima lowered two sleeping bags and two thermos bottles, one of tea and one of soup, to the stranded Japanese. He then climbed down to the camp below, reaching it about 10:30, where he found everyone asleep, or as he said, pretending to be asleep. He was unable, he said, to persuade members or Sherpas to mount a rescue effort until the morning. The men were finally rescued, some 24 hours after their fall, but their hands and feet had frozen and they later lost them.

1964 was also the year in which Jimmy Roberts kicked off the trekking business. Nima asserted that he, Danu (our cook), and Nima Dorje were the three original Sherpas with Mountain Travel.

> ...after you left in '63, you remember, all the expedition tents and tables, chairs, you left here. (JL: I didn't realize that) Yeah, cost too much money [to send it back to U.S.]. Doesn't worth it. What's the point? And they give for us, left Jimmy Roberts. So, then after you left, then we went with you to the United States. After we come back, we tried to use some kind of name, is Mountain Travel. So we tried to request the government, but they say, What do you mean, Mountain Travel? Nobody heard about it before. So, [we said] Mountain Travel is people who walk the

> mountains, by feet. That is called Mountain Travel. And then say, Yes, they will give the Sherpas the permit. So at that time we had no sleeping bags. So we got the cotton blanket, and we had no double bags, so we bought the big rice bags. We put two or three blankets in the rice bag, we keep using, I think we used about three years, and after Jimmy made a little bit of money, and we bought sleeping bags in Germany. ... Tents, sleeping bags, everything.

One of the treks Nima led sounded special; as it turned out, it changed Nima's life.

> And I take care very well for them. I didn't follow the normal travel routes I want to, different track, different route. Putting completely different place, they like to have the quiet treks. Not noisy treks. So we look the good water place, we camp the jungle, ... and after we finish the trek we reach the Pokhara. Then the guy says, I want to ask for something for you, which you like, you know. And I didn't know what he was saying, you know. Yes, I like very much, what you offer for me? And he called me, he said, I like to offer the job for you. All your family, going back in the States.

The man making this extraordinary offer was an industrialist, and before that a scientist, who Nima says was involved in the invention of both the "black box" that airliners now carry and also a World War II bomb-sighting device. The job he had in mind for Nima was taking care of his large house in Baltimore, Maryland. Nima tried it for 18 months, to make sure he could do it and that life in Baltimore was livable, and then brought his family over.

The wife of his benefactor was an established artist who maintained a second house in France, and she frequently took Nima and family there. The wife suggested the second child, a son, should be born in the United States so as to have citizenship here, but almost as soon as he was born the whole family was back in France, where they remained for six years. Nima experienced the schoolroom for the first time in Paris:

> They put me in French school, so, at that time it was all the people who should go, like diplomatics, have to go to French language. So, I'm not diplomatic, but I interested. So I went to school, they paid everything, it's quite expensive. And I was in, you heard about it, the Salk vaccination? Dr. Salks? We were same class. Two years we spent together. Amazing. I'll tell you, at that time I was feeling so shamed myself , 'cause I was too old to learn those things. And after I went to class, people 50 years old, 45 years old, from Russia, China, all places coming to learn in that place, then I'm feeling much better (laughter). And then, I said, if they can learn, I can learn (laughter).

He intended, he said, to emigrate permanently to the United States. By his own account what happened to divert him was that an old friend of his bought the Nepalese jungle resort called Tiger Tops, and begged Nima to come back to work for him. By the complementary account of an American who knew him then, what happened was that the relationship with his original benefactor soured and he needed something like the return to Tiger Tops to get himself out of it. In any case, all returned to Nepal.

After several years of working in the resort and also taking treks out from that base, Nima says friends encouraged him to set up his own trekking operation, which he did, sometime around 1975 (the numbers don't work out very closely in this story but it didn't seem important enough to get it exactly straight).

> I haven't sold one shoelace [from expeditions and treks], I kept all my equipment, I just buy cooking utensils, some tents, but the rest I had, sleeping bags and boots and all. And the government come to estimate how many people you can run, I can run 45 people per day. So they give a license for me. ... Then before I don't have this

big house, I was always booking the hotels. OK, hotels are not really comfortable, sometimes group shows up sometimes they don't. ... So, then, all my friends advised, build a bigger house. What do you need, hotel? We don't like to stay hotel. Even we stay hotel, we come here. We love to have the family home, see the culture, see the living things. And the hotel, 50 people living in the one hotel, we don't know each other. We have not one conversation, we learning nothing, they say. So finally, extension, bigger house.

His two children are both at the moment living in the United States. The older, his daughter, is married to the son of another of the AMEE Sherpas (Ila Tsering, who was with us on the '63 Sherpa tour). This son, Tsering Wangdi, is just finishing his medical training and is probably the first Sherpa to receive a medical degree in the United States. In a way, it was Tsering Wangdi who launched me on my quest to find our Sherpas. I had never thought of them in any context other than the expedition, and it was startling to hear about one of the second generation going so far with his education. It led me to the question, What has been going on here?

Nima's second child is a son. He finished high school in Kathmandu and has been working with his father's trekking agency ever since.

Nima's story is worth summarizing: what we have here is a onetime yak-herder who by the time he was 40 had climbed high on Everest, trekked all over Nepal, toured the United States, lived in Baltimore and in Paris, in Montparnasse and on the Champs-Élysées, fathered an American citizen, and started his own business. Nima could hardly be called representative, but he is perhaps the best example yet of the dramatic changes in some Sherpa lives.

> 3/8: I'm not very good being alone this long. Losing my motivation for new experiences. And, too much sitting around, making difficult connections. Is it worth it? (But also, do I have anything better to do? What's really bugging me?) I think I'd do better with a more focused, definable (achievable?) project. Also, the cooing of 100 pigeons in the courtyard is driving me nuts!

I had asked Nima if he could take me to the monastery outside Kathmandu where Kalden now lives, but he promised instead to bring Kalden to his house for a meeting.

Kalden, Kathmandu

Kalden is a man of slight build with a smile of benevolence that never disappears. He seems to be continually blessing the world, as though all that he sees around him is good and beautiful. Of the Sherpas that I met, he is either the man most at peace with himself and the world or the man who most wants to appear at peace. I prefer to assume that it was genuine peace. His wife died four years ago and he returned to the life of a Buddhist monk, which he had left many years before. He is now the head monk in a small monastery, the goal of his life apparently to prepare himself for dying well, although that event is not likely to be at hand; Kalden appears well and happy.

He astonished and dismayed me by bringing me a gift—wasn't it enough that he made a two-hour round trip just so that we could meet?— and the gift was a bottle, doubly expensive in Nepal, of Red Label scotch whiskey! Once again I felt the guilt of the undeserving.

Kalden understood some English, but we needed Nima Tenzing as interpreter. I've already indicated that I found Nima's English often difficult to understand, so getting a picture of Kalden's life was as difficult as getting that of Nima himself.

Kalden was born in Tibet, probably in the early 1930s, but grew up in Namche Bazar. Through Nima he told me that he remembered little of his childhood, and in fact the tone of the whole interview suggested that he has no interest in looking backward at this point. His eyes are on preparing for his reincarnation.

His father was a Buddhist monk, and Kalden took this route himself as a young man. Sherpas who obtain a certain level of Buddhist education can, in effect, set themselves up as monks and offer their services in the community for carrying out rites and rituals as required. They need not live in monasteries. This appears to be how Kalden and his father lived and worked.

Somewhere around 1960, or when he was close to 30, Kalden "let go the monks" (as Nima put it), got married, and went to Darjeeling to look for work. I couldn't tell whether or not this break came from dissatisfaction with life in Khumbu, as it had for so many of our other Sherpas, nor whether or not his ambition was climbing, but the story seems to be that he took courses with Tenzing and Gombu at the HMI and then became an instructor there. Through HMI he was hired as sherpa on Cho Oyu, one of the major Himalayan peaks

(26,760 feet), and in 1962 went to Everest with the Indian expedition which failed to make the summit by only a few hundred feet.

On Everest again in 1963, with AMEE, Kalden carried loads three times to the South Col. On his third trip he was carrying supplies for the summit effort of Lute Jerstad and Barry Bishop, and several days later Lute wrote about this carry: "The Sherpas [who included also Pemba Tenzing and Nima Tenzing] were just fantastic, carrying about 70 pounds without oxygen." But Kalden ran into trouble, as Lute told his diary: "Several hours ago Kalden began complaining of pains. He was breathing hard. ... Barry and I both thought, Oh, boy, here we go again with another bad case of pulmonary edema. We got out the P.E. [pulmonary edema] kit to be on the safe side."

They found that giving him oxygen made things much better and were able to avoid using the kit. The next morning Lute wrote: "Kalden still has those chest pains. I'm sure it's a case of carrying too much too high. He has simply had it! We are sending him back down with another Sherpa."

That was the end of Kalden's high-altitude load-carrying in 1963. In 1965 he was back on Everest with another Indian expedition, undoubtedly recruited by Gombu through the HMI. This was the same expedition on which Gombu made his second trip to the summit.

I believe it was soon after this that Kalden moved from the HMI to the Indian Mountaineering school in Sikkim, where he became a colleague of Ang Dawa's. I learned that Kalden had also participated in the joint Indian-U.S. "special project" to put an electronic sensor high on Nanda Devi, and in fact had climbed to the summit of Nanda Devi three times.

Kalden remained with the Indian school in Sikkim until fairly recently, instructing and leading training expeditions toward the Chinese border. By staying in India rather than returning to Khumbu, as so many other Sherpas had, he gave up the option of making money as an entrepreneur. Instead, like many of the rest of us, he was content with a salary and the promise of a pension. He seems to have retired about the same time his wife died. They had one daughter who was raised and educated in Sikkim and today works in a bank in Darjeeling, where he visits her often. A quiet, peaceful, lovely man.

> 3/10: Flight around mountains was disappointing, didn't go in over Namche. Wind looked pretty strong over Everest. Flew at 19,000, and I had guessed we were at 27,000. Perspective. Young girls near me using Everest as a backdrop for pix of each other! Did get great sense of how all the landforms fit together, from river valley to high peaks. No compelling emotion, just a quiet sense of awe at the effort I'd once put out, and a satisfaction in getting a comprehensive view.

CONCLUSION
FROM ALISON

As I mentioned in my introduction, Dad wrote no conclusion for this manuscript. At the end of the Kalden section, however, there is a four-sentence paragraph that feels like a note to himself on final thoughts. The questions it contains are quintessential Jim Lester, representing an honesty beyond which he wasn't convinced there was much to say. I'd bet he was unwilling to undertake an effort to manufacture a concluding chapter without an editor saying he had to and showing the way. Dad would have called it "blather."

Here it is:

Should I have stayed longer in Nepal? Should I have spent more time with the Sherpas I found, dug deeper for insights into their lives? These are questions that won't go away, and I fear I may not have done a thorough job of dispatching my "unfinished business." But I'm unlikely to go back again, and for better or worse this will have to do.

I'll not blather either. Instead, I'll leave you with an extra note

Dad made at the end of his journal on June 4th, 1998, a few months after his return home:

> I just looked at the poster over the fireplace and it seemed pregnant with meaning (2 glasses of wine with dinner). And I realized that all through this project there's been the secret hope that somehow, through it, I'll break through to a great meaning. This may well be what was putting me in a strange state when I was there, with the feeling that something should be happening that wasn't. One thing that comes to mind is my memory of how I felt when I read that whoever wrote "76 Trombones" had incubated it for decades, until finally it all came together and he was able to flower with it. So I think I've harbored the secret fantasy that one day all the seemingly unrelated threads of my life would come together into a beautiful fabric that I could proudly display to the world. What a load to impose on any project I might undertake! No wonder I felt odd in Nepal! I got a bit free of it when I got down to coping with the trail, and later when I got down to coping with writing. But I suspect it's creeping back into the writing project, and I want to use it as a vehicle to bring out all the strong and beautiful thoughts I've had that there's been no way to express -- no context, no structure. Dangerous fantasy!

RETURN TO THE SCENE OF THE CLIMB

The poster over the fireplace. Drummer boy, Kathmandu 1963

FURTHER READING

The most recent addition to my shelf of related books is *SHERPA: Stories of Life and Death from the Forgotten Guardians of Everest*, published in 2022, by Pradeep Bashyal and Ankit Babu Adhikari, who so kindly agreed to read this manuscript and offer their reaction to it. In their energetic way, it picks up after Dad left off.

My constant companions throughout the development of this book have of course been *Everest: The West Ridge* by Thomas F. Hornbein and *Americans on Everest: The official account of the ascent led by Norman G. Dyhrenfurth* by James Ramsey Ullman and other members of the expedition. To read about the study Dad did of the climbers, turn to his contribution to the book, chapter 14.

James Ramsay Ullman also aided the writing of Tenzing Norgay's autobiography, in some editions titled *Tiger of the Snows*, in others *Man of Everest*, published in 1955.

Dad refers several times to the writing of Wilfrid Noyce. The book he quotes from is *South Col: The personal account of one man's adventure* on Everest, published in 1954, after Noyce's participation in the British Everest expedition.

Writer and environmental conservationist Broughton Coburn took another in-depth look at AMEE in his book *The Vast Unknown: America's First Ascent of Everest*, published in 2013. Coburn also helped Jamling Tenzing Norgay, son of Tenzing Norgay, to write *Touching My Father's Soul: A Sherpa's Journey to the Top of Everest*, published in 2001.

In 2018, California State University lecturer and director of the Vulnerable Landscapes, Resilient Peoples project, Philip W. Clements drilled down into what the scientists were engaged in on the climb in his book *Science in an Extreme Environment: The 1963 American Everest Expedition*.

If you're intrigued by the CIA's Cold War operation to drag a nuclear-powered listening device to the top of Nanda Devi to spy on the Chinese, get yourself a copy of *An Eye at the Top of the World: The Terrifying Legacy of the Cold War's Most Daring CIA Operation* by Pete Takeda, published in 2007.

If you're more interested in what makes some American climbers tick, read the 2019 memoir *My Old Man and the Mountain* ("what it was like to 'grow up Whittaker'") by Leif Whittaker, son of Jim.

Pasang Yangjee Sherpa's doctoral dissertation, *Sherpa Perceptions of Climate Change and Institutional Responses in the Everest Region of Nepal*, Washington State University, 2012, is available to read via the rex.libraries.wsu.edu website.

ACKNOWLEDGMENTS

I have had the privilege of roping some extraordinarily helpful, knowledgeable, and patient people to me for this climb.

Tom Hornbein, thank you for being my long-term friend, sounding board, fact-checker, cheerleader, and master of useful introductions.

Dr. Pasang Yangjee Sherpa, thank you for raising my awareness in so many ways and giving me your ear so often at a punishingly busy time in your life.

Dr. T. Wangdi Sherpa, son of Ila Tsering, son-in-law of Nima Tenzing, and the first Sherpa to receive a U.S. medical degree, thank you for your excitement upon hearing of this project, and for the chance to double-check so many names and relationships with you.

Mary Ann Frye, thank you for your enduring interest, and the ice-ax keenness of your questions and proofreading.

Andy Gurnett, thank you for the hours you spent removing the dust from digitized slides, designing such a strong cover, laying out the book so beautifully, brainstorming with me, and calming my internal turmoil.

Return to the Scene of the Climb, and I, would have been lost in the foothills without you all.

ABOUT THE AUTHORS

James T. Lester was born in 1927 and raised in St. Louis, Missouri. He was awarded a PhD in psychology and philosophy from UCLA, and worked as a clinical psychologist, teacher, and research administrator in the United States, Germany, the US Virgin Islands, and England. He published numerous articles in the field of psychology, ranging from his Everest study to military psychology to organizational stress. He was also a gifted jazz musician and arranger, and in 1994 Oxford University Press published his biography *Too Marvelous for Words: The Life and Genius of Art Tatum*. He died in 2010.

Alison Jean Lester is a novelist. With a BA in Chinese and French and an MA in Chinese studies, she spent 25 years in Asia, studying, working, writing, and raising her two children, before settling in England in 2016. She is the author of the novels *Lillian on Life*, *Yuki Means Happiness*, *Glide*, and *The Sound of It*, as well as the short-story collection *Locked Out: Stories Far from Home*, and a memoir about the ends of her parents' lives, *Absolutely Delicious: A Chronicle of Extraordinary Dying*.

Dr. Pasang Yangjee Sherpa is a Sherpa anthropologist from Pharak in northeast Nepal. Her research topics have included Indigeneity, human dimensions of climate change and the Sherpa diaspora. She is currently Assistant Professor of Lifeways in Indigenous Asia at the University of British Columbia.

Tom Hornbein pioneered the West Ridge ascent of Mount Everest with Willi Unsoeld in 1963, and is the author of *Everest: The West Ridge*. He became a member of the University of Washington School of Medicine faculty in the departments of anesthesiology, physiology, and biophysics upon returning from Everest, and from 1978 to 1993 he served as chair of the Department of Anesthesiology. He lives in Estes Park, Colorado, the place where he first met mountains.